From
Schlub
to Stud*

From Schlub to Stud*

How to Embrace Your Inner Mensch and Conquer the Big City

*Max Gross

Skyhorse Publishing books may be purchased in bulk at special discounts for sales promotion, corporate gifts, fund raising, or educational purposes. Special editions can also be created to specifications. For details, contact the Special Sales Department, Skyhorse Publishing, 555 Eighth Avenue, Suite 903, New York, NY 10018 or info@skyhorsepublishing.com.

www.skyhorsepublishing.com

10 9 8 7 6 5 4 3 2 1

Library of Congress Cataloging-in-Publication Data

Gross, Max.
  From schlub to stud : how to embrace your inner mensch and conquer the big city / Max Gross.
     p. cm.
  ISBN 978-1-60239-263-2 (alk. paper)
  1. Conduct of life--Humor. 2. Men--Humor. I. Title.
  PN6231.C6142G76 2008
  818'.607--dc22
                              2008012939

Printed in the United States of America

To my parents—who never loved me enough!

Zhlub
Zhlob

Pronounced ZHLUB or ZHLAWB, to rhyme with "rub" or "daub."
From Slavic: *zhlob*, "coarse fellow."

1. An intensive, ill-mannered person. "He acts like a *zhlub*, that *zhlub*."
2. A clumsy, gauche, graceless person. "Vassar-Shmassar, the girl's still a *zhlub*."
3. An oaf, a yokel, a bumpkin. "What can you expect from such a *zhlub*?!"

A Jew came running into a railway station, the perspiration pouring down his face, panting and crying, "Stop, train, stop!"
A *zhlub* said, "What's the matter?"
"I missed my train!" the man exclaimed. "By twenty measly seconds!"
"The way you're carrying on," said the *zhlub*, "one would think you missed it by an hour!"
See also KLUTZ, BULVON, GRAUB.

—Leo Rosten, *The Joys of Yiddish*

Table of Contents

Introduction

Not too long ago, I went out on an assignment in Brooklyn with a photographer. There might have been something forlorn or melancholy or just plain exhausted about the look on my face because as I slumped down in the passenger's side of the photographer's van, he said, "Max, you look tired."

A week earlier, my girlfriend had told me that she didn't think our relationship was going well. "I really do love you," she said, "but sometimes you can love a person and just not be able to live with them." I collected the sundry shirts and books I had left in her apartment, put her keys down on the kitchen counter, and bid her farewell. "You should call me in a week or so," I said, "and we can discuss this further."

I never heard from her again.

"What's been going on?" the photographer asked innocently, unaware of all that his question was about to unleash.

How was I going to start? It wasn't just that my girlfriend had broken up with me. That was, indeed, bad. (We were serious enough that we had discussed a future wedding and children.) Nor was it the fact that I was sleeping on my parents' couch, which made it worse. Not that my parents were bad people. Difficult, certainly (as these pages will attest), but hardly bad. But after a certain age, living with one's parents has the unsavory taste of failure.

But there was something else, too, which was shameful and difficult to talk about, as if I was admitting to being a sex offender or having a venereal disease.

"My apartment has bedbugs," I announced.

That was the reason I had moved back in with my parents. And it was at least part of the reason my girlfriend had broken up with me.

The photographer—who was an extremely likeable and laid back southerner of the Owen Wilson variety—suddenly stiffened.

"Really?" he said quietly.

"Yeah," I said. "And last week I broke up with my girlfriend."

The photographer started the car and we drove along in silence for a few moments.

"Wait a minute," the photographer said. "Didn't you also just get audited or something?"

Oh, yes. I might not have mentioned that. The previous November, I had gotten the letter from the IRS requesting an examination of my expenses. I had spent much of the winter sifting through receipts and credit card statements and making desperate late night phone calls to my best friend, who is a lawyer.

"Yeah," I said.

The photographer's eyes went wide for a split second and then he broke into an unfettered laugh.

"Max," he bellowed, "you're in hell!"

And for the first time in more than a month, I didn't feel like screaming or weeping. For that brief, fleeting moment, I actually felt good. Because I—like many baffled patients before me—finally had a diagnosis.

Yes, I was in hell.

These were the dark days of schlubdom.

I have a syndrome, you see. It can alternatively be called "feckless-ness" or "cluelessness" or "haplessness." But for the purposes of this book, I will call it "schlubbiness." I am a world-class schlub, and at that particular moment, being a schlub felt like a curse.

What is a schlub? The basic definition, as I see it, is this: Some-one a little unkempt. A little out of shape. A little clumsy. A little gauche. A little insulated. A little bookish. A little too enchanted with Woody Allen and Philip Roth. (Oh, and *The Simpsons*.) A lit-tle daunted by the outside world and all its demands. And, finally, a little luckless. (Like, they probably won't print this book.)

I have made numerous questionable decisions over the years—sometimes professionally, sometimes romantically, and certainly stylistically—and they all felt as if they were conspiring to run my life off the tracks.

I couldn't help but feel that if I had been a little savvier with women, things wouldn't have spun out of control with my girl-friend. If I had been a little more organized and rigorous with my expenses, I wouldn't have been audited. If I had kept a neater apartment, it wouldn't have been infested with bugs.*

But, having since reflected on this at length, I think I was being much too hard on myself.

Being a schlub isn't all that bad. In fact, I think you will dis-cover, as I have, that it has definite advantages. Yes, that rotten

---

* It's not, as my mother insisted, a biblical *plague* for slovenliness, by the way. As you will see later in the book, bedbugs have little to do with how messy or neat you are. They attach themselves to people unlucky enough to get in their way. But I can't say that I didn't feel deeply that the bedbugs were my fault.

spring was a definite low point for me—but as time went on, things started to improve greatly. Two years later, I am not unhappy. I owe the IRS no money. I have a hot girlfriend. I have a bug-free apartment.

In that time, I don't think I've gotten significantly less schlubby. In fact, I've grown to embrace my schlubbiness.

Fellow schlubs: You have nothing to lose but your *zitz*. In fact, you have reason to celebrate. Being a schlub is desirable. Hopefully, I will show you how to make life work a little bit *smoother* through the suggestions and observations in this book.

For non-schlubs out there, here is the ultimate primer on the weird and unkempt people you encounter on the subway or meet in a bar. You might find us a little too disorganized and unserious, but I think you can learn something from us, too. While life is certainly a serious business most of the time, I often think it is taken way too seriously. A schlubby indifference to stupid minutiae can liberate you from stress.

In the summer of 2007, when the movie *Knocked Up* came out, I (and all the other schlubs I knew) nearly wept for joy. With a big, lumbering galoot like Seth Rogen as the public face of our movement, the whole world could now come to appreciate the benefits of schlubbiness. True, the Rogen character in *Knocked Up* was a man who was not equipped to deal with the world—and he needed a level-headed Katherine Heigl to steer him away from the rocky shoals—but he had a great, bottomless heart.

The women in the movie theater were actually tearing up at the end. An impoverished, puffy-haired, chunky Jew suddenly seemed like saint and sex god.

There are literary antecedents to the schlub-as-heartthrob; in the nineteenth century, the Russian novelist Ivan Goncharov produced a great book called *Oblomov*, which presented the most lovingly detailed portrait of a schlub ever created. Oblomov, the eponymous hero, is sort of a comic version of Hamlet—the question he wrestles with is not "To be or not to be"; it's, "To get up, or not to get up." *Oblomov* is an ode to sloppiness, laziness, and numerous other human flaws. But it's also about the joy of an interior life. And I think Franz Kafka, Isaac Bashevis Singer, John Cheever, and other great writers saw the wild literary possibilities in men whose tangled heads are somewhere other than their bodies. *Knocked Up* is very much in that tradition.

This was very good news for me. More than just looking like an unkempt schlub, I bore a startling resemblance to Rogen—down to the puffy red hair, the broad shoulders and the well-fed belly. People stopped me in the street and asked me if I was, in fact, Rogen. (Or a relative.)

And that was the inspiration for the book you are now reading.

From Schlub to Stud*

Chapter One*

*Looking the Part

"Almost all neatness is gained in man or woman by
the arrangement of the hair."
   —F. Scott Fitzgerald, in a letter to his
      sister Annabel

There's an old Gross family story that when I was about two or three years old, my mother took me to a trendy children's store called Malawi and the Mighty Mole and when she asked me what clothes I wanted, I exclaimed:

"I want fashion!"

The words were music to my mother's ears.

Some mothers may have been worried. After all, what does it say about the future sexual preference of your son if he's a fashionista at age three? (Not that there's anything wrong with it.)

Other mothers would have brushed it off as the sort of cute thing all toddlers say when they're three—every linguistic tick and mistake is adorable at that age. But my mother was a fashionable woman who knew a thing or two about style. Her grandfather had been a tailor who spent his professional life in the ladies garment industry, and even though she had long since opted for a career as a writer and editor, her grandfather's ghost remained firmly perched over her shoulder. When she took a job at the holy grail of professional journalism, *The New York Times Magazine*, it was as an editor for the style section. She spent her days poring over pantaloons and fabric swatches.

So I imagine that after her initial shock wore off ("I want fashion!" is seriously weird even by toddler standards), she must have felt something akin to awe. Fashion had been coursing through her family's veins, and now her three-year-old showed the family colors!

I sometimes feel sorry for my mother when I think of this, now.

More than a quarter of a century has passed since that afternoon, and I'm fairly certain it was the last time I really cared about fashion. In fact, you could say that I developed something of an aversion to it. When I tell people that my mother is the executive editor of *T*, *The Times*'s style magazine, I am oftentimes met with a sideways glance, as if to say, "Your poor mother." Some day I expect to be called a liar.

And I also feel sorry for my mother, because she has worked so earnestly to make me overcome this apathy towards clothes.

Starting at around the time I went off to college until the day this book was published, my mother had been on an endless campaign to get me to dress better, to get slimmer, and to please (*please!*) put gel in my hair.

"Don't you want a girlfriend?" my mother has pleaded with me. "Don't you want to be happy?"

Well, sure I did.

"You don't understand, Max," my mother has said, "and take this from me because I know: Girls are really, really superficial. It's true. You could be F. Scott Fitzgerald and it wouldn't make any difference. They want somebody who dresses well. They want somebody who doesn't look like they just rolled out of bed. They want somebody who doesn't have holes in their sweaters and in their pants. And the sad truth is, they're not going to even talk to you if they don't like what they see."

And, yes, I admit it: I have walked around with holes in my sweaters. (I've even shown up for work in such a garment.) I own trousers the cuffs of which are ragged from dragging along the floor; I have other pants with cuffs that are so high that you can see my socks (which, I am told, is extremely uncool). And my hair looks as if it has never touched a comb.

I have a problem that I have no control over, and I need help. But like many other people who need help, I have long reconciled myself to the fact that it is a losing battle. I was born an ungroomed, sloppy dresser. I'll likely die that way.

But my mother has refused to give up. There's a kind of Ralph Nader-like purity to her quest into making me less of a schlub. (At least dress-wise.) The phone calls are unrelenting. As are the offers for shopping sprees at Banana Republic where she'll pick up the tab. ("Just promise me you'll throw away those khaki pants with the hole in the knee.") Or free haircuts at trendy, East Village hot spots. ("Just promise me you'll use gel afterwards.")

"Max," she said to me one evening over the phone, "what if I could get you a spot on *Queer Eye for the Straight Guy*? Would you go on?"

Normally, when she says such things, I have a tendency to humor her. "Sure, Ma," I'll say and promptly forget about it. And when I thought about it later, I didn't see how she could secure me a slot on that show anyway. For one thing, I'm not quite as frighteningly nerdy as the guys who generally appear on *Queer Eye*. Moreover, my lack of style, I think, comes more from a sense of ambivalence about style than seriously bad instincts. And I still can't think of anybody she knows at the Bravo network who could manage to pull off such a large favor.

But my mother sometimes has an iron sense of determination. Who knows what strings she'd pull and favors she'd call in? I could be exposing myself to the whole world as a hopeless slob. And even though I like to think of myself as a reasonably good sport (who would be willing to have a little fun made of myself if it was an interesting enough experience), I was having none of it.

"No, Mom," I said. "I'm not going on *Queer Eye for the Straight Guy*."

For a long time, I didn't realize I was a slob. (Or, more accurately, I didn't realize I was quite so grand a slob.) Sure, every once in a while I would see some ghastly photo of myself—hair jutting out in all different directions—and agree that it was time to get a haircut. But, mostly, I was comfortable with the way I looked. I believed that my mother's nagging was standard for any Jewish mother. (Hadn't Philip Roth made a very beautiful living describing the antics of one such mother? And my mother wasn't anywhere close to Sophie Portnoy's level of nuts.)

You could even say that I was proud of my offbeat hairstyle. I'd had a bad experience with short haircuts, you see. When I was eight or nine years old, I was studying myself in the bathroom mirror and decided that my hair was getting too long and there was one clump of hair in particular that "just had to go." With all the forethought of the Bush Pentagon, I picked up a pair of scissors, grabbed an enormous handful of hair, and cut.

The hair fell to the sink, and I stared at a big empty patch just above the right side of my forehead.

Even to my untrained, unfashionable eyes, this did not look good.

But nine-year-olds are generally optimists, and I figured that there was a decent chance no one would notice. After all, I couldn't have told you the first thing about my friends' haircuts. I was certain they weren't paying attention to mine. I put down the scissors, flushed the incriminating tuft of hair down the toilet, went back into my room and proceeded to forget about my impromptu haircut for the time being.

An hour or two later, when my mother came to tuck me in and give me a goodnight kiss, she leaned over me and froze.

"Wait a minute," she said.

There was an uneasy moment as her eyes scanned over my face. She knew that something was off, but for a few seconds could not quite figure out what it was. Then came the scream:

"What did you do?"

"Oh," I said, downplaying as much as possible. "I was fixing my hair a little . . ."

Without another word, I was marched into the bathroom and made to look in the mirror. There it was. Bald spot. A big one. Smack in the front of my hairline. And my mother was too dumbfounded to speak.

Instead of speaking, my mother began brushing my hair over the bald spot, in some vain attempt to cover it up.

"Oh, my God," she murmured just loud enough for me to hear her.

Then she called my father into the bathroom and—as a family—we all stared at the wreckage that had become my head.

"Well," my father said, assessing the damage, "I think we're going to have to take him to a barber."

"Of course we're going to take him to the barber!" my mother said, now at full volume. "The question is whether they're going to have to cut all his hair off!"

"All my hair?" I said, chiming in for the first time.

"There's no other way it'll be even," my mother said. She looked at the reflection of me in the mirror again, and again began brushing my hair with her hands to try to mold it into something acceptable. "I don't think there's any other way."

A few days later, I was taken to a barber near Bloomingdale's whom I asked, with a tremendous amount of sincerity, if he could save the basic bulk of my hair. As I looked up at him, I tried to look as meek as possible—like a combat veteran asking if his leg could be spared. (If the barber couldn't save my hair, I wanted to be damned sure he felt bad about it.)

The barber studied my head for a few seconds before he informed me, "I'm sorry. It'll all have to be cut off. Otherwise it'll grow in all wrong."

And so all my reddish-golden curls were coldly, mercilessly lopped off.

I sat in the barber chair seething with horror and revulsion.

For one thing, this haircut made me look chubby. Not that I hadn't known somewhere in the back of my mind that I was over-weight (for more on this, see Chapter Eight), but my chubbiness suddenly made itself apparent in a glaring, undeniable way. And, second, I looked like a complete and utter dork—like I had just stepped out of a 1950s soda shop. A crew cut? What kind of 1980s child wears a crew cut? I was a savvy enough kid to know I didn't want to associate myself with that square era.

For the next few weeks, I wore a cap around school that I ada-mantly refused to take off under almost all circumstances. I at-tended birthday parties in the cap. I went to the park in the cap. I played basketball in the cap and ate dinner in the cap. I think that the only times I took it off were when I showered and slept (and I might have even tried to wear it to sleep, but my father told me that hair grew faster when it was uncovered).

Come to think of it, there was only one other time I would take the cap off: Every few hours I would go into the bathroom and stare at my baldness for a few minutes, hoping that there was some sign that my hair was returning. Of course, it was an achingly slow process. For weeks, I would just shake my head and agonize over what I had been thinking. "Why?" I kept asking myself. "Why?" Over and over again, I vowed never, ever to get a haircut that short again. Ever.

After my hair grew to a respectable, Elliott Gould-in-the-1970s-length, it became my trademark. I was the kid with the hair.

It puffed out and grew wild and big (but, in a rebuke to gravity, never fell to shoulder length). And when I became a teenager, it only became bigger. Walking around high school, I resembled a funky, 1970s disco impresario. Thankfully, I attended an extremely hippie-dippy school where I was far from the only oddball running around.

A couple of years ago, I came across a book by a guy who billed himself as a maestro of picking up girls; I wasn't dating anyone at the time and thought it would be a funny idea to write an article about the guy, using myself as a test case for his advice. We met up at my apartment in Brooklyn one evening, and his first words to me were:

"Get a haircut."

A day or so later I obliged him, but I felt like a traitor doing it.

My style of dress was a much less emotional issue.

I don't think I became an out-and-out slob (dress-wise) until college.

College has a way of doing that to people. Even though I went to Dartmouth—which attracts a staggering number of J. Crew shoppers—the whole institution of higher education brings a man's inner schlubbiness to full bloom. It makes sense, in a way. When you're arriving at class at nine in the morning and you're still drunk from the night before, you think about your appearance a lot less than you did when you lived with your parents. When the other males in your calculus class are unshaven and smell of beer and reefer, you begin to feel classy if you took a shower that day. And when you were awake until 5 AM finishing a philosophy paper on the vast difference between "a priori" versus "a posteriori" reasoning in Kant's "Prolegomena," you probably couldn't give less of a shit if your pants were sagging when you dropped the essay off at your professor's office.

Moreover, college is the one place where being a slob is somewhat respectable. The fraternities at Dartmouth were the most foul smelling, messy, decrepit structures I have ever set foot in. (And I've visited halfway houses in East New York.) During my tenure as an undergraduate, the Alpha Delta house (which never got tired of boasting that they were the inspiration for the movie *Animal House*) was declared an open sewer by the town of Hanover. But despite this, the AD guys were considered extremely cool. (Which separates them from schlubs.) As were the other rowdy (and malodorous) frats. The Dartmouth girls didn't seem to mind being pawed by guys in shorts, shower shoes, and backwards baseball caps.

By these standards, I was a snazzy dresser.

My clique of hipsters and schlubby Jewish intellectuals might not have been outfitted at Barney's, but we certainly weren't any worse than the Alpha Deltas.*

So I never felt the necessary pressure to keep my wardrobe spiffy. Trousers developed holes in the knee, and it didn't seem like a particularly big deal. (I certainly didn't think I needed to throw them away.) A stain would appear on my favorite sweater and after treating it with soap and water, it never occurred to me that I might also want to drop it in the washing machine or take it to the cleaners.

In a sense, my mother might share some of the blame for this: I grew up under the impression that I was of a brand of Semitic royalty. When I opened my dresser in the morning, my clothing was

---

* I'm not sure you can join a cool frat and still be a schlub, but I'm pretty sure you can get away with being a hipster-schlub.

cleaned and neatly folded—and I never bothered to figure out how this happened. If I really thought about it I could have told you, yes, there was a dry cleaner on Montague Street that my mother visited fairly frequently. And, oh yeah, there were those two big washing machines in the basement that sucked up quarters every week. But I was a Jewish prince, and princes don't think about stains and laundry and dry cleaners.

However, when you're off on your own for the first time, this takes a while to sink in. By the time I left college, I had developed a respectable number of bad habits.

The difference between me and the other Dartmouth slobs was that my bad habits never seemed to go away. They only intensified.

Part of this has to do with the fact that most of my friends jumped into Wall Street jobs or law firms after school where dress was corporate, and they were immediately getting the kind of money where they could afford to outfit themselves in sharp clothes. Another part has to do with the fact that I moved to Israel for a year after college where clothing descends to a new level of "casual." (I once went to a wedding in Jerusalem where I was one of only two males wearing a tie—and the other male was the groom.) Also, I had a kind of reverse snobbishness about fashion. I fancied myself an intellectual who was above such mundane, worldly things as trends and brands. Really, who—besides a doting mother—cares about such nonsense?

And finally I started in possibly the most casual (read: schlubby) profession known to man: journalism. Where the standards of dress can be extremely loose.

It took a heart-to-heart with one of my editors at my first job before I realized that my sense of style was bad, even by reporter standards.

"Max," said the news editor at *The Forward* one afternoon, "do you have a minute to talk?"

"Sure."

We found an empty office.

"You might want to consider dressing better," he said.

I was thrown off guard by this. Granted, I had heard this over and over again throughout my adulthood from my mother, but it was the first time I had been confronted in a professional setting. I felt a little like a drunk who had been caught in the men's room with a flask of whisky.

"Really?"

"If you want people to take you seriously, you should," he said. "Go buy yourself some new pants. And you shouldn't wear sneakers all the time. Also, you might want to try a tie." (Over the course of the conversation he also told me that I should cut down on the number of calls I made to my father during working hours. "I hear every word of it," he told me. "We all do. And it's a big distraction.")

I went home completely stunned. "You should take this to heart, Max," my father advised. "When you dress well, people will start treating you better. Watch. You'll see." So the next morning I showed up in wingtip shoes, a dry-cleaned shirt, a pair of black slacks, and a tie (I stopped short of putting any products in my hair)—and that would become my standard outfit until I left *The Forward*.

It felt highly unnatural.

So now that you know a little bit of how your narrator has dressed the part, you might be wondering if you, too, are a schlub. Well, there's no simple formula. But there are a number of telltale signs. These are some of the warning signs.

You might be a schlub if . . . there are only three shirts that you actually wear.

Go to your closet or your dresser and take a look at your wardrobe. If you've only been wearing two or three different outfits every week, you might be on the road to schlubbiness. There are only three pairs of pants I ever wear—and only one that I wear consistently. Plus, of all my button-down long-sleeved shirts, there are only one or two that aren't straight black. Extra points if one or more of your standard outfits has a hole in it.

You might be a schlub if . . . when the light bulb in your reading lamp blows out, you switch chairs.

It's such a simple thing to change a light bulb that you might wonder "Why not do it right away?" The schlub will reply: "If it's such an easy thing to do, why does it need to be done right away?" At least, that's the mentality I have. As I write these words, there are currently two light bulbs that are burned out—one in the hallway, one in the dining room. I have no plans to replace them any time soon.

You might be a schlub if . . . there is anything alive in your refrigerator.

I once kept rice pudding in a big Tupperware container in the back of my refrigerator from late December until early February. After a while, I was too afraid to remove the container. Every time I opened the fridge I would see it with a sort of dread. Who knows what was living in there.

You might be a schlub if . . . you threw out said container.

A schlub, or a coward anyway, but there was no way I was cleaning that.

You might be a schlub if . . . you don't know who Kevin Federline is.

Or, more accurately, if you don't give a shit who K-Fed is. It took me a long time—a very, very long time—to remember the name of Britney Spears' ex-husband. (And I work at the *New York Post*!) but let's face it: Schlubs couldn't care less about this sort of stuff. It took me a month before I figured out what everybody was talking about when they kept mentioning Janet Jackson's wardrobe malfunction.

You might be a schlub if . . . your photo ID has expired.

When I am asked for photo ID at a bar or an office building, I can only hope that whoever's checking it doesn't look too hard. I never learned how to drive (yet another sign you might be a schlub), and all I have to identify myself is a learner's permit that I got when I was sixteen. It expired about a decade ago.

You might be a schlub if . . . you are always meaning to buy a big package of "Sorry I'm late with your birthday" cards to keep around the house, but can never get around to it.

Because, let's face it, a schlub can never remember a birthday on time. Thank God for e-cards, right?

You might be a schlub if . . . you've never figured out how to send an e-card.

I'm told it's a very simple process. And I sincerely hope to get around to figuring it out one day.

You might be a schlub if . . . you still think *The Big Lebowski* is hilarious on the eighty-seventh viewing.

There are a whole other canon of dumb movies that we schlubs love and adore (and repeat lines from) ad nauseum: *Old School*; *Harold and Kumar Go to White Castle*; *Dude, Where's My Car?*; and *Zoolander*. The best of the bunch is *Lebowski*. A true schlub will never tire of it.

You might be a schlub if . . . you're reading this book.

You might be a schlub if . . . you hate Jeff Foxworthy. What. A. Schmuck!

Chapter Two*

*Finding a Vocation

"A writer is compelled to undertake a certain amount of thinking. It does not have to be much."

—Philip Wylie, *Generation of Vipers*

There are days when I have wondered what life would have been like if I had become, say, a doctor instead of a writer.

I'm fairly certain I would not have been happy.

Of course, there are plenty of happy doctors out there. I'm sure that every shapely brunette that these guys approach in a bar is duly impressed when she asks him what he does for a living, and he coolly responds: "Vascular surgeon." In one fell swoop, he has informed her that he's bright enough to survive medical school and financially solvent to boot. Without doubt, a glint appears in the girl's eye.

And I'm sure that most doctors feel pretty good when they gaze at themselves in the bathroom mirror. People who spend their life keeping their fellow human beings alive and healthy don't have those panicky moments of self-doubt when they whisper the unbearable words: "I'm wasting my life."

No, doctors never say that kind of thing.

And, yes, I'm sure that I'd also feel a certain glib satisfaction if I walked into a party filled with investment bankers and lawyers and was able to think to myself that if one of these glorified clerks should suddenly succumb to a heart attack, I would be their only chance at survival. I would be the gatekeeper between them and eternity. All their earthly riches would be worthless in comparison to my medical degree. That would, indeed, feel pretty good.

But there are very few doctor schlubs. (Unless we're talking about one of the more innocuous sorts of doctors like podiatrist or chiropractor—for more on this, see the sidebar.) For one thing, being a doctor demands too much precision. You can't *almost* save a guy's life. You can't come up with the *second-best* diagnosis. You can't perform a flawed, but fascinating operation. Doctors deal in absolutes. Schlubs thrive on life's shades of gray.

I would have been much too nervous to be any good as a doctor. I would have been the bane of every insurance company out there: I would order tests for everything—even the things that don't hurt; I would completely overmedicate my patients; I would phone patients six months after they had come into my office to check up on them. "Are you absolutely *sure* you're feeling okay?"

"Yes, Dr. Gross," they would reply. "My cold has gone away, I assure you." My hands would tremble during every operation. I could see myself, midway through a complex procedure, stopping everything as I turn to the nurse and ask: "Did I wash?"

In short, I would have been a disaster.

Writer, on the other hand, feels like the kind of profession that was invented to accommodate the nerdy and hapless in the world.

A writer's life, as I imagined it, consists of sitting alone at a desk (or in a Starbucks, if you're so inclined) and coming up with stories. Philip Roth once described it as a life dedicated to "turning around sentences." Dress code is flexible. As are working hours. And all the time you spend goofing off reading anything from Dostoevsky to *Maxim* magazine, can legitimately be called research. Writing can at times be extremely boring and frustrating (I've always believed Leonard Cohen's song "Waiting for the Miracle" was about writing) but it can also be exhilarating when it gets going. Henry Miller spent his entire professional life recounting his sexual conquests. You could do a lot worse.

You certainly don't have to worry about whether or not you washed.

Unfortunately, it's a difficult profession to break into. The number of short story writers who actually make a living off their stories can be counted on the fingers of one hand. Novelists or writers of nonfiction can do somewhat better, but before you can actually afford to live on your own as a novelist (and not in your parents' basement), you have to sit down and squeeze out a real novel. One that is publishable. One that strangers will actually pay money to read. (Your mother can only buy so many copies.) Even those happy few who have managed to make a living off it rarely make a good living. Most people I know who have undertaken this lonely art have to supplement their income as either a teacher, paralegal, office manager, or journalist. (All of which, incidentally, are pretty good jobs for schlubs—except for the office manager.)

I toyed with the idea of becoming a teacher for a while. In fact, when I started college, I assumed that graduate school and a professorship lay some place in my future. But by the time I finished my bachelor's degree, I was utterly sick of higher education. I had come to the conclusion that my professors were—by and large—insufferable. Literary theory has a way of draining any and all joy you might take in books, and the successful students were the ones who bought into theory completely and loved to preen their obscure knowledge of post-structuralism before the class.

Plus, I couldn't stand the political correctness you have to deal with in university life. I took a twentieth-century British fiction course where we didn't read a single word of Somerset Maugham or P.G. Wodehouse or Rudyard Kipling, but we did manage to fit in Michael Ondaatje's *The English Patient*.

Strictly for the birds.

"Forget about graduate school," I told my parents. "I'm going into the Peace Corps after school. That, or I'm moving to a kibbutz in Israel."

I moved to Israel, and after a year of "seeing the world" and "experiencing life," I came back to New York and began considering which of the three jobs besides teacher I would take to supplement my dream job as a writer.

A friend of mine was an editor at *The Forward*, a weekly Jewish newspaper, where I had spent a summer interning. I asked her if I could just sort of show up, get my byline in the paper every week and learn the ropes as a reporter (getting paid only for the articles I published).

"Sure," she said. "Come in on Wednesday. Or whenever you like."

Oh, my!

Even as I think back about that statement years later, I have to swoon in thinking how casually—how schlubby!—it all began.

I was living at home at the time and temping other days. So it seemed like a good way to learn the business.

Having now spent some time as a journalist (and having since moved over from a small Jewish weekly to one of New York's big dailies), I have come to one big conclusion: Journalism is perhaps the greatest repository of schlubs known to man.

Of course, not every journalist is a schlub. I'm sure that there are plenty of men and women who cover the United Nations or the stock market or wars in the Middle East who are impeccably professional in both their approach to journalism as well as their approach to life. *The Wall Street Journal* and *New York Times* are chock-full of decently dressed overachievers, whose desks are not littered with random scraps of paper, and who sincerely believe they are engaged in a kind of social service and feel a great sense of responsibility to the newspaper reading public. Had Seymour Hersh gone to medical school, I'm sure he would have done very well.

But they're not the kinds of reporters I hang out with.

And despite all their pretensions to the contrary, even places like *The Times* are infected with unmitigated cases of schlubbery at every level. I happen to know people at the paper of record who dress as badly as I do. Whose social skills make me come off like George Clooney by way of comparison. And have you ever seen the *Times'* former Baghdad correspondent, John Burns, interviewed on Charlie Rose? Dude, his afro is about as unwieldy as mine. There's no question that John Burns is a schlub.

But the real place to find the schlubs of journalism is in the tabloids and small ethnic papers.

My colleagues have included men and women who graduated with the highest honors from Harvard and Yale, and people who never went to college at all but who can rattle off obscure policy decisions made during the Eisenhower administration and offer the most trenchant analysis of a story you've ever heard. (My father is one such reporter.) Many of them are biding their time as they toil on the great American novel. They occasionally come to work shrouded in Hawaiian shirts or ratty sweaters, and they reek of marijuana. But they could come up with headlines that would have you laughing on the floor. (Hilarity is not a criteria to be a journalist. But it certainly helps at a tabloid like *The Post* or *The Daily News*.) They can stop you in your tracks when you read some sort of shocking story they've uncovered. They'll casually mention some old favorite book you thought nobody else in your generation had read.

Most editors don't care that these reporters lead dysfunctional social lives, so long as their copy is on time and (mostly) mistake-free.

Plus, journalism encourages a kind of dilettante approach to the world. A reporter has to learn a little bit about a lot of different things. If he gets to be too expert in one specific field, he goes off and writes a book, but few of my friends in journalism have done that sort of thing. Most reporters I know have switched around from beat to beat over the years. They can tell you a great deal about genetic research. Or the impact of the subprime meltdown on the larger stock market. Or why the Sadr army is aligning itself with Iran's Revolutionary Guard.

In other words, journalism is perfect for someone who doesn't have the patience to stick to one thing.

It sounded about right for me.

My first job, at *The Forward*, was not a straight reporter's job—I was hired as the personal assistant to the editor-in-chief, and I was allowed to do some reporting on the side.

In a world of schlubby newspapers and reporters, *The Forward* is among the schlubbiest. (Which I say with a great deal of affection; if anyone is pro-schlub, it's me.) It started out as a socialist paper—and it was originally written in Yiddish. The great Yiddish writer Isaac Bashevis Singer first published his stories and novels in *The Forward* before they were translated into English and sold to magazines like *The New Yorker* or *Esquire*. At the beginning of the twentieth century, *The Forward* was something of an institution; it had more than a quarter of a million readers and it came out daily. (My ancestors, however, felt *The Forward* was too right wing for them—they went with the more stringently communist Yiddish newspaper, *Die Freiheit*.)

When I got to *The Forward*, it was still being published in Yiddish on one side of the building, and it was published in English—as a liberal Jewish weekly—on the other side of the building. I worked on the English paper. And it proved a very strange place to learn the ropes.

The reporter's part of the job was interesting enough, even though 90 percent of my reporting had to be done over the phone.

(As an assistant, and de facto office manager, I could never leave the office for any long period of time. I would also have to interrupt phone interviews in midstream to answer the editor-in-chief's line whenever it rang.) I did stories about a *dybbuk* that supposedly possessed a fish in New Square, New York. And a piece about a guy who was trying to single-handedly start Jews for Allah (in the same vein as Jews for Jesus).

But just as interesting (probably more so) was my life as an office manager, which everyone should do at least once in life if only to learn a little humility.

Aside from the editor-in-chief's phone, I answered the general line to the office; when somebody called and nobody quite knew who to send them to, they were routed to me. As small as *The Forward* is (there are roughly 26,000 readers), the phone never stopped ringing.

The majority of the calls were simple requests for our fax number or our email address. Or a request for an old copy of the paper. (I was a soft touch, who granted nearly all requests, free of charge.) Most of the callers were a good thirty or forty years older than me (sometimes much more), and the callers needed to be delicately walked through things like *The Forward*'s web site. But occasionally I would get wild, angry calls that were filled with venom and bile.

Answering phones for a newspaper is a good window into the almost mystical power most people still assign to the written word. So many people called me expecting justice. The funniest (and most heartbreaking) calls were from people to whom some cataclysmic wrong had been committed, and who were expecting the press to leap to their defense.

"The government sided with my ex-wife in our custody battle because I'm Jewish," one called told me.

I immediately assumed the guy was a lunatic.

The Forward couldn't afford to alienate its readership, however, and I was expected to be reasonable and polite with everyone. I told him I would speak to the editors about his plight.

Thereafter, he and I developed a friendship of sorts. He faxed an endless parade of legal documents to our office, and he would call me to make sure that they had arrived safely. We would then discuss his case (he would tell me the latest developments) or we would just chat with each other as if we were old friends. "So, what are you working on this week, Max?" he would ask.

As we chatted, I began to wonder if, in fact, he *wasn't* the victim of some sort of anti-Semitic conspiracy.

There were other calls of a similar nature, but sadder.

An Orthodox Iraqi Jew phoned me in a state of profound despair. For several weeks, he repeated to me the lengthy list of financial misdeeds that had been committed against him, and the heartbreaking number of family members who had abandoned him over the years. Ordinarily, I would have told him right away that his story (way too complicated to be restated, or even understood) was not suitable for publication and that he should try his luck elsewhere. But there was something in his voice that worried me. He would sign off on our phone calls saying in a heavy, thick accent: "This is all I have left—you doing a story about me."

I wondered if he was going to kill himself. I went to the managing editor and asked his advice on what to do.

"Give him the number for the suicide hotline," the editor said.

A reasonable response, I suppose.

There were calls of such childish naivety that I can only laugh when I think of them now. (And they annoyed the hell out of me at the time.) One woman called up and said that we should send a reporter out to interview her because she had just witnessed a miracle.

"What was the miracle?"

"I have this Magen David that my daughter gave me," the woman said. "For the past twenty-five years, I have not taken it off. Not once. The other day I went to Daffy's to try on some clothes, and when I got home, the Magen David was gone. I couldn't believe it. It was a gift, I loved it so dearly; I was so sad. The next day I retraced my steps. I went to Daffy's and tried on all the clothes I tried on yesterday. And as I'm trying on a blouse, I feel something in the sleeve . . . and what do you think it is? The Magen David! Now, if that isn't an act of God, I don't know what is."

I had to stifle a laugh.

"Well, that's an amazing story," I said. "It's not the kind of thing we'd send a reporter out to interview you for. But you should write it up as a letter and send it to us."

I was a little stunned to find out later that, yes, *The Forward* printed her letter.

And finally, there were the angry calls. I had to field hundreds of calls from cranky old Jews who told me that *The Forward* had become unforgivably right wing. I fielded other, similarly angry calls from infirmed men and women who told me that *The Forward* was a left-wing rag and self-hating in its criticism of Israel. "I'm canceling my subscription and never renewing it! I don't want you to deliver that paper to my house any more . . ." One reader threatened to report me, personally, to the State Attorney General's office (I think he lived in either New Mexico or Arizona) if he ever received another bill from *The Forward* again.

There were complaints about the stories we ran, the stories we didn't run, about typos and about errors. I fielded them all. And in those days, I couldn't quite decide whether I had the best job at the paper or the worst.

The most persistent—and loony—of my regular callers was the widow of a well-known Yiddish poet. The widow is still alive, and extremely litigious in her dealings with the outside world. So for the sake of my finances, I'll just say that her name is Irma Gottfried.

She called me one pleasant, spring afternoon, and without missing a beat she was ready to do battle.

"Who am I speaking to please?" Mrs. Gottfried said in a thick, Eastern European accent the moment I picked up the phone.

I told her.

"Mr. Gross," she said, "I am the widow of Yakov Gottfried. You know who Yakov Gottfried is, no doubt."

I did not.

She was eerily silent when I told her this.

"You work at *The Forward* newspaper, and you don't know who this is?" she said.

"Sorry."

Her husband, I later found out, is indeed considered by many to be one of the greatest Yiddish poets. I have also since read his poetry (and one or two stories) in translation and failed to be impressed. Not that he was bad, necessarily. And one young Yiddish scholar I know insisted that Gottfried's prose is much more elegant than Isaac Bashevis Singer in the original Yiddish. But I am not convinced. Gottfried is somewhat limp in translation.

"Anyways, Mr. Gross, there was an absolute falsehood in the story you published about Yonatan Ellstein," she continued. "You know this story?"

I did not.

Another silence.

When she spoke again, it was in a patronizing tone of voice, as if she were speaking to a simpleton. "What is your position at *The Forward*?"

"Assistant to the editor-in-chief."

"And who would I speak to about this?"

"Me."

She sounded annoyed. But she nevertheless swallowed her pride and asked me to pass along her complaint to my boss, J. J. Goldberg, *The Forward*'s editor-in-chief. She then proceeded to tell me her outrage:

In a profile we had run that week of the Canadian Yiddish poet, Yonatan Ellstein, the eighty-nine-year-old Ellstein was asked who his literary influences were and he said: The late, renowned Yiddish writer, Yakov Gottfried, who was "a bosom friend and like a brother or father to me."

"Yonatan Ellstein was a mediocrity who does not deserve to be mentioned in the same sentence as Yakov Gottfried," Mrs. Gottfried said to me. "He was not his bosom friend." Her husband—if Mrs. Gottfried is to be believed—barely knew Ellstein and looked down on him and whatever piddling writing talent he had.

To make a long story short—and her phone call lasted fifteen to twenty minutes—she demanded a retraction.

"Okay," I said. "I'll discuss it with the editors."

And before signing off, she asked me to look up her husband in the *Encyclopedia Judaica*. I promised her I would and was thereafter content to forget about it.

She called a day later and asked to speak to my boss. It was a Tuesday or a Wednesday when we were putting the paper to bed and I asked her to call back. She did. And again. And again.

"Why don't you write a letter?" I suggested. "We can put it in the letters section."

But for some reason, that idea didn't go anywhere for some time.

She kept demanding to speak to J. J., the editor of the paper. And although I was expected to humor everybody who called, part of my job was to shield J. J. from lunatics like Mrs. Gottfried. I denied all her requests.

For the next few months, I fielded dozens of calls from Mrs. Gottfried. And the months did not dissipate her sense of outrage; she was almost always just as angry when the phone call started as she was on the first phone call. But—as with other repeat callers—I developed a sort of friendship with her, too. She would ask me if I had looked up her husband and she was positively thrilled when I did. She was thrilled when I told her the name of one of her husband's short stories that I had read. She suddenly became a little grandmother—beaming with pride that I had gotten a gold star from my teacher.

Every phone call was, in many ways, the same. She would reiterate how great her husband was, and how scandalous it was that we had printed what we did. Why hadn't we called her for a comment? Why had we just accepted Ellstein's word?

"You can't check every word of every article," I said.

Mrs. Gottfried became a bit of a joke around the paper. As she hounded me over the weeks and months, I would fill my fellow writers and editors in on the latest phone call, and they would alternate between shaking their heads in bafflement or laughing uproariously.

"Mr. Gross—Max," she would say to me (after our first few conversations I told her to call me by my first name). "This is a libel. And I have contacted my lawyer who assures me that we can bring suit against *The Forward*."

Lawsuits were taken seriously at *The Forward*.

Early in my tenure, I nearly resigned when an article of mine was spiked because of a possible lawsuit. As one editor put it, "We're not *The New York Times*. We can't afford to have a lawsuit." But, then, that's the newspaper business. Every few months our main political correspondent sat in J. J.'s office and discussed his articles with *The Forward*'s lawyer over a conference call. I would bring the legal bills down to the accounting office afterwards, and I knew just how much they hurt.

When Mrs. Gottfried began talking of a lawsuit, she was instantly taken much more seriously.

I remember sitting with J. J. and the managing editor as we discussed it: Was it possible? Was this ridiculous quote really something we could be sued for? "If we were repeating a libel, it's absolutely actionable," J. J. said.

Would this woman go so far as to spend hundreds of thousands of dollars to prove that her husband was not friendly with an inferior writer? (But, I wondered, what else does she have to do?)

The tone when speaking about Mrs. Gottfried suddenly got drearier.

One day I was impersonating Mrs. Gottfried's latest demand to a colleague (and I could imitate her fairly well) when the president of *The Forward* walked by. He called me a few minutes later.

"I just overheard you, Max," he said, angry. "This is a very serious case. This woman has threatened us with a lawsuit. And as long as you're acting as J. J.'s assistant, you shouldn't be discussing his personal business with anybody."

It was an implicit threat. Schlubs do not react well to threats (we tend to shrivel away). So I kept my mouth shut after that.

But Mrs. Gottfried did not disappear; when she saw that she wasn't making sufficient progress with me, she tried another tack. The Yiddish circle was small enough at that point so that no one could really ignore the widow of Yakov Gottfried. She began phoning Harold Ostroff, the chairman of the Forward Association (who has since died) and began haranguing him.

One afternoon, a slip of paper from Harold appeared on my desk that I was asked to pass along to my boss.

"Dear J. J.," the note read, "Please get Irma Gottfried off my back . . ."

J. J. drafted a letter to Mrs. Gottfried in which he asked her to stop calling Harold, and to speak to him, directly.

The next time she called, I put her through to J. J.

It was decided that J. J. and Mrs. Gottfried would draft together a two-hundred-word letter refuting Ellstein's claim. One Thursday morning, the two of them hammered it out over the phone. When they finished, J. J. handed me a sheet of paper and said with a sigh: "Fax this to her lawyer."

From that moment until it went to press, Mrs. Gottfried was calling me two to three times per day.

"Mr. Gross—Max—would you please read the letter to me?"

I would read the letter and she would stop me halfway through.

"Please, Mr. Gross—Max—would you underscore the word 'not?'"

"I'll ask J. J."

"Okay, now would you read it to me again from the beginning, please?"

I brought Mrs. Gottfried's request to J. J. "Tell her no," J. J. said, handing the letter back to me.

I nearly cried.

I could picture a kind of nightmarish back-and-forth (something I was never very good at) with Mrs. Gottfried upon telling her no. And I was tempted to do her bidding for her and say, "Oh, please, J. J., what possible difference could it make?" But he was the boss.

The next time Mrs. Gottfried called, she asked: "Is the word 'not' underscored?"

"I was going to call you about that," I said. "I spoke to J. J. and he said no."

"Oh, well," she said.

I was so stunned at how calm a reaction she had that I didn't even mind reading her the letter twice more.

"Where is the letter on the page?" she asked.

"I don't know."

"Mr. Gross—Max—please do me a favor. Please don't let them put it on the bottom of the page in the corner. This is an important article. Please put it on the top of the page—or in the middle."

I promised to pass her request along to the layout people.

Mrs. Gottfried called to ask me what the headline would be. When she heard the headline—"Friendship Refuted"—she was thrilled. "Oh, Max!" she cried. "Please tell Mr. Goldberg that I said he is brilliant. That is the perfect headline!"

I passed along Mrs. Gottfried's compliments. J. J. shrugged.

When the paper finally appeared, Mrs. Gottfried called me to thank me for my help. And I was extremely glad everything was more or less over. I briefly wondered what Yonatan Ellstein would say if he saw the paper—but, then, not everybody who's profiled in the paper really reads *The Forward*. Not that he would care nearly as much as Mrs. Gottfried appeared to care.

Several weeks after her letter had been published, Mrs. Gott-fried called me again. She was just as angry as she was in the first few days I had spoken with her.

"Mr. Gross—Max—I read the editorial in the last issue of the paper," she began, "and this is absolutely outrageous . . ."

I was suddenly terrified. Terrified, and extremely pissed off. Had some reporter or columnist actually been stupid enough to mention Yakov Gottfried somewhere in print?

And as she plunged into her denunciations and her usual spittle of outrage, I mentally began drafting an interoffice memo. "Under no circumstances shall the name Yakov Gottfried appear in *The Forward* unless it is first checked and approved by J. J. Goldberg. Any reporter or editor who knowingly violates this rule will auto-matically be forwarded Irma Gottfried's phone calls."

But this latest complaint was genuinely confusing. And Mrs. Gott-fried was phrasing things strangely. After a few minutes, I couldn't follow what she was talking about so I stopped trying to pay attention. I checked my email and began straightening out my desk.

She ended fifteen minutes later by saying that she was faxing something over and would I pass it along to J. J.

"All right . . ."

Five minutes after I hung up, a twelve-page fax started coming through, and Mrs. Gottfried called to make sure I had received it.

"Mr. Max," she said, "read me what you have."

I told her what we had received and she began barking.

Usually, when I tuned Mrs. Gottfried out, I would insert little "uh-huhs" into the conversation to at least keep up the appearance that I was paying attention. I was too much of a schlub to speak rudely to her (most schlubs are polite), but I wasn't about to make any effort to hide my annoyance this time. I didn't say a word.

"What's wrong, Max?" she finally asked. "You sound upset. You don't sound like yourself."

"Well, frankly, Mrs. Gottfried, I don't know what you're talking about."

"What do you mean?"

"I lost a strand in there, and I haven't been able to get it back," I said. "What exactly is the problem?"

"Well, why didn't you stop me?" she asked. "I'm trying to *teach* you something."

To translate what she said into something understandable it was basically this: She was upset that we had referred to a certain writer as a "Great Yiddish writer" in one of our editorials.

"Who did we say was a great Yiddish writer?" I asked.

"The Nobel laureate!" she cried. "How many Yiddish Nobel laureates are there?"

I took a moment to think.

"Wait a minute," I said, "do you mean Isaac Bashevis Singer?" The line was silent.

"I would never say that name out loud," she hissed.

And she proceeded to heap insult upon insult on Singer as a pornographer, as a self-hating Jew and a believer in devil worship. (If you want proof of how the Yiddish literary world seethes with jealousy over the only Yiddish-language writer to win a Nobel Prize, read Cynthia Ozick's great short story, "Envy.")

Such, such are the joys of working at a schlubby newspaper. But then, that's the nature of being a journalist. You speak to a lot of nuts. And, yes, that teaches you something about the world. But I embraced it; it was a pretty funny story to tell to the girls in the bar.

Obviously "writer" is a good job for a schlub and surgeon is a bad one. But there are lots of other professions in between. So here's my personal guide to the top five best and top five worst jobs out there if you think you're a schlub.

Five Best Schlub Jobs:

Sidekick: Ed McMahon made a pretty good living by sitting next to Johnny Carson and letting Johnny talk. He never had to say anything all that pithy, and he never had to keep himself all that buff—he just needed to feed his boss straight lines. And Ed did it profoundly well. Paul Shaffer does it remarkably well, too (albeit with slightly more musical talent than Ed). It shows how far a schlub can go being a sidekick. But the sidekick is not merely the domain of the talk show; sidekicks abound almost everywhere. And with good reason; they provide a necessary sense of contrast. Whenever a politician gets on a podium to announce some new bill or initiative, there is always some rumpled-looking advisor standing next to him or her. Suddenly, standing next to somebody who doesn't look so good and who doesn't say anything too interesting and who doesn't look as if he could get a table at a nice restaurant, well, you come out looking much better. (Political consultant is the intellectual equivalent of sidekick. David Axelrod? Schlub. Mark Penn? Big schlub.)

Rabbi / spiritual leader: If you can get through learning Hebrew, rabbi is one of the greatest schlub jobs out there. (Although this really extends to leadership positions within almost all organized religion.) You sit around all day reading books. Then, every week, you come up with an opinion on everything you've read, and your congregation has to listen. Jews, for one, have an extremely weird (and endearing) respect for people who change their minds; you can give a sermon one week on the importance of keeping kosher and the very next week say how unimportant the kosher rules are next to, say, charity and being kind to others. There's no single correct answer to any of the big questions out there, so you always have room to justify your flip-flops. And the more Orthodox you get, the less emphasis is made on your style of dress—which is perfect for a schlub (if you've ever been to a synagogue in Williamsburg, you know what I mean).

Personal injury / criminal lawyer: Back in the 1960s, a man named William Kunstler proved that you could be a total schlub and nebbish and still be a kick-ass lawyer. (He also invented the comb-over-anchored-by-a-pair-of-glasses-on-your-forehead look, which was picked up by Gloria Steinem.) Ron Kuby, Barry Scheck, and countless others have just gone further in proving this correct. There's nothing we schlubs like better than to argue. A schlub can be quick on his feet. And schlubs can be quite charming. After all, you're not trying to get the jury to date you. Just to decide the case for your client. This is one of the more lucrative schlub jobs out there. Negative: law school.

Genius: Albert Einstein and Bill Gates have done more to cement the genius-as-schlub image in the popular mind than I ever could. They climbed to the top of their scientific fields, but they never felt the need to dress up to do it. Why should they? They were thinking of more important things than haircuts and dry cleaners. In that sense, the schlubbier you are, the smarter people assume you are. You might consider telling people you're a genius.

Ice cream flavor inventor: There are dangers associated with this kind of job for a schlub. You might be tempted to invest a little too much of yourself in the work. (See Chapter Eight, on diet.) But it is, nevertheless, a profession a schlub would do very well in. For proof of this, I only invite you to take a look at Ben Cohen and Jerry Greenfield—two schlubby hippies living in Vermont who got the brilliant idea that if you like ice cream, and you like cookie dough, maybe you could combine the two for one great super-ice cream. Hence the birth of their ice cream label, Ben & Jerry's.

Five Worst Schlub Jobs:

Investment banker: You will spend your life surrounded by complete schmucks who will judge every aspect of you on the basis of where you buy your clothes and what neighborhood your apartment is in. If you're a true schlub, you stand no chance of ever earning their respect. And you wouldn't want to. Some people might get a rush trading tens of millions of dollars, and coming out richer on the other end, but these people are generally to be avoided and despised. Most schlubs won't feel comfortable trading those kinds of figures. If you should happen to lose it, well, you won't feel good afterwards. (For a more complete rundown on why I-bankers are insufferable, watch the underrated comedy *American Psycho*.)

Dentist: Much like surgeon, this is one that requires way too much precision—as well as too much willingness to inflict pain. I don't think a schlub could hover over some terrified person's open mouth with a dozen sharp instruments, doling out jabs and pricks and scrapes and be able to call himself a schlub. (To be a proper schlub, you need to be a somewhat benign personality. Dentist requires a certain streak of sadism.)

Army officer: Well, this one shouldn't be tough to figure out. A few years back, I told a friend that I could never get into the army because of the fact that I have flat feet. Should you go into the army (mistake number one) and test well enough for them to want to put you into officer school, one of two things will happen: You will be completely cured of your schlubbiness (and, hey, maybe it really wasn't for you); or two, you will commit some sort of elaborate suicide like Vincent D'Onofrio in *Full Metal Jacket*. Either way, soldiering is a profession schlubs should avoid.

Social worker: I have a great deal of sympathy for social workers out there. My sister is one; she's dedicated her life to helping the disadvantaged. And I've heard stories from social workers that are endlessly touching. But it's a job that allows for very little joking around. (All the social workers I know take themselves very seriously.) Social worker is a little like doctor—you're delving into ruinous lives and trying to do damage control. If you work with abused children, you might wake up one morning and find that one of your children stabbed seventeen people. And even though it's not your fault, you will feel more guilt than a schlub can handle.

Engineer / architect: In any Woody Allen movie, there is always at least one character who is described by his friends as "brilliant" or "a genius." The character in question is invariably an architect. Woody isn't the only one who does this; screenwriters love to make their lead character an architect. I think the reason has something to do with the fact that it's unquestionably a brainy profession, but you also need an artistic eye as well as style and taste. In short, it's way too cool for a schlub to undertake. Plus architect—like engineer—demands a certain amount of practical competence that a schlub just can't muster. Your bridge can be one of the most beautiful designs ever conceived of . . . but it can't fall down. Maybe it's better left to the non-schlubs of the world.

Chapter Three*

*A Room with a Jew

"To be parted from your house, your father's house—
it oughtn't be allowed. It is worse than dying."
—E. M. Forster, *Howard's End*

Some time during college I made a frank determination about myself: I am not a particularly good roommate.

Schlubs rarely are. (Unless they are paired with other schlubs. Even then, they should really only be put in an apartment big enough not to drive the other schlub crazy.)

I'm sure that all my former roommates will feel a great sense of vindication upon reading this. Well, they're entitled. I'll say it once more, definitively:

It wasn't you—it was me.

But it took me a while before I came to accept this. Nobody wants to think that he is cranky (or smelly) in the morning. ("Why is *he* always so goddamned cheerful?" you say.) Nobody wants to believe that he is a complete and utter slob. ("I've got a system!" you roar when your roommate tries to push your stacks of paper that have piled up in the living room out of sight.) Nobody accepts that he shirks off his share of household chores. ("I mean, really, what's the big deal about getting the dishes washed this very second?")

In short, nobody feels that he is a horror to live with.

However, most of the bad roommates I've met (schlubs and non-schlubs alike) have constructed elaborate fortifications against admitting that they, in fact, are the guilty party. (I have a friend who managed to drive three roommates from her room over the course of one year of college, and yet she is still offended when I joke around that she might not have been an ideal roommate.)

But let's speak honestly, fellow schlubs: We are the ones who keep the place a sty. We are the ones who make all sorts of noises at all hours (biological as well as other). We are the ones who stay on the phone way too late and are constantly forgetting to turn off electrical appliances as well as burners.

I think part of this has to do with the fact that I grew up as a de facto only child (my half-sisters are much older, and I never really lived with them). When you have a big room at the end of a large New York apartment all to yourself, you grow accustomed to your privacy. Even as a kid, I hated having my solitude disturbed.

Summer camp was always one of those jarring events that had to be endured rather than savored. Never mind that summer camp is one of the worst possible experiences for a schlub (schlubs don't do well with woods, ticks, sunshine, hiking, and all the other outdoorsy nonsense that camp entails); the fact that I had to live with other children drove me into conniptions.

I hated the music my fellow children listened to (there was a big Guns N' Roses fan in one of my cabins); I hated the political opinions of my fellow campers (I was always stuck with at least one admirer of Ronald Reagan and George H. W. Bush, and I was not a particularly open-minded ten-year-old); I hated the communal "lights out" rule where you couldn't stay awake and read; I hated the cramped little cots you had to sleep on and the narrow showers that smelled of mildew; and I really hated not having a television and video collection at my beck and call.

In short, I couldn't wait to get away from camp and back to the comforts (and air conditioning) of my family apartment in Brooklyn Heights.

College wasn't much better.

My freshman year, I was paired with a fairly nice guy named Michael from Bethesda, Maryland, in an ugly, single room not much bigger than a prison cell on the far outskirts of campus. (The cluster of dorms—called the Choates—was generally considered the worst housing on campus.)

Michael and I were moderately friendly for several weeks; we ate a few meals in the dining hall together and made the rounds at the sundry frat parties on the weekends. But after a while, I think we both realized that our pairing had been a mistake. Not that Michael was a bad guy—not at all—but we didn't have much to say to each other. The fact that our beds were only about ten feet apart without a wall—or any barrier of any kind—made everything just a little bit worse than it needed to be. (In retrospect, I'm not sure why it never occurred to either of us to go out and buy a Japanese Shoji screen, or something. Lesson learned, I suppose.) And we both said and did all sorts of things to get on the other one's nerves.

For one thing, Michael was an even bigger slob than I was.

When I filled out my housing forms and it asked if I was generally messy or neat, my mother said: "Don't you *dare* say that you're neat."

From an ethical standpoint, she was right, of course. But (as I said in Chapter One) I was a relatively neat person by college standards. And when you're paired with someone who is an even bigger slob than you are, it tends to bring out the nagging impulse in you. One day when I was complaining about the mess in our room, Michael said (quite rightly): "Hey, don't lay this on me. I said on my housing form that I was messy."

Touché.

He was a smoker, and even though he didn't smoke in the room, I couldn't stand the cartons of cigarettes that were littered on the floor.

And I think my sense of humor and general manner was a little too brusque for Michael. I once referred to Ronald Reagan as "a senile old fuck," which drew an extremely indignant response. (Unbeknownst to me, he had a grandparent with Alzheimer's Disease. My phrasing did not sit well.)

I knew nothing about computers at the time (I know only slightly more now), so I was always asking him some sort of question about Microsoft or email, to his continued annoyance. "I'm going to do you a big favor," he said to me one evening when I asked him how to double-space a document, "I'm not going to tell you. Figure it out yourself. You'll thank me." (I groaned in impatience, and just called one of my other computer-literate friends instead.)

I don't remember quite how our living situation came to a boil (it might have been over the Reagan comment) but it did. "I think we need to talk," he said. So we sat down one evening and went over our problems together. Michael acted grown up and conciliatory; I was defensive.

"It's just a place to hang my hat," I told my friends afterwards.

Next year, I took a room by myself and decided to do without a roommate all together. It was a little lonely, but I figured I was better off lonely than angry and fighting all the time.

I didn't try a roommate again until I was a senior. I'm not sure who suggested it—whether it was my best friend, Dave, or me— but when the idea of living together came up, it sounded like a good one. David was another New York Jew who shared my misanthropic sense of humor and had a simpatico view of the world. We were sharing two rooms instead of just one. And he was fairly easygoing, someone who I knew wasn't interested in making my life difficult.

"We'll be fine," I told my mother. "No reason to worry. None at all."

Our cohabitation lasted peacefully for about two months before it started falling apart. David found an extremely affectionate (read: horny) girlfriend, and the two barricaded themselves in his room for hours at a time. I would come home at night to find the suite dark, David's door closed with low techno music pulsing on the other side, and a squeaking sound coming from his futon.

I suppose I can't blame him. I'm sure if one of my relationships back then had lasted more than two consecutive weeks (or two consecutive dates) I, too, would have been as noisy as possible, just in case anybody in my dorm didn't know that I had a girlfriend.

But at the time Dave's frolicking infuriated me to no end.

On the few occasions when I decided that I wasn't going to be kicked out of my room and barreled in anyway—squeaky bed noises be damned—I slammed the door loudly, flicked on the lights, and was as deliberately noisy as possible, just to let them know that I could hear everything. Sometimes (rarely) the noises would stop. But it wouldn't be long before I would hear the hushed moans of David's girlfriend and the squeaking would start up again. "You're fooling yourself if you think you're going to get any studying done," I would say to myself. "You're also fooling yourself if you think that they give a shit that you're in the room."

I would shuffle off to the library, or one of Dartmouth's many lounges, or upstairs to my new best friend's room to bitch and complain.

Dave and I eventually had it out, too. One afternoon I invited him out to lunch and told him that he and his girlfriend were spending too much time in our room, and why weren't they using *her* room? (Especially since her room was empty.) We both became upset (the manager of the coffee shop came to our table to quiet us down), but at the end of our heart-to-heart, David agreed to use her room on occasion and we shook hands. (It felt like a puny victory.)

We finished the year not as close as we began it, and somewhere over the course of the year, I vowed to do whatever was in my power to never have a roommate again who wasn't a potential wife.

It makes sense that schlubs—who are, by definition, a little messy and a little clueless about the minutiae of life—would make for shitty roommates.

However, a schlub can do fairly well when living in his parents' house. (Only a parent can tolerate a schlub.)

At least that's what I found after my post-college year of slumming around Israel.

When I came back, I had no intention—none whatsoever—of finding an apartment. At least not right away. For one thing, I wasn't making enough money to support myself on my own. In those days, I would pick up $300 per week as a temp, and if I was lucky I would make another $200 or $300 for an article in *The Forward*. (But, then, *The Forward* didn't pay you until a month after publication.) In a city where it's tough to find an apartment for less than $1,200 per month (even in a marginal neighborhood), that wasn't the kind of salary I could hope to live on.

"I'll just stay here until I find my sea legs, right?" I said to my parents.

I'm sure they felt that they couldn't say no. When I was in Israel (which was reeling from the Second Intifada), I toyed with the idea of applying for citizenship and staying there permanently, much to their perpetual horror. They spent the year begging me to come home (making all sorts of hints about their willingness to pay for graduate school or helping me out financially if I would just return). So I guess that they figured if getting me back to America meant putting me up in their apartment for a few months, so be it. They weren't necessarily happy that their five years of freedom from their son were coming to an end, but they weren't about to put me out on the streets, either.

And even though nobody is exactly happy about the idea of being a fully grown adult—and a graduate of a prestigious university—who lives with his parents, I found that it wasn't really so bad.

I was still an incredible slob (and my parents still actively criticized this quality), but I was never allowed to make their apartment too disgusting—a cleaning lady came every Tuesday. And although non-native New Yorkers have a tough time believing this, my parents' apartment was one of those massive old New York apartments that ran 1,800 square feet, had two bedrooms, a den, a living room, a dining room, two bathrooms and a separate kitchen. It was the sort of home where you really could avoid members of the family for long stretches of time if you were fighting with them. (When my girlfriend's cousin—who's from Oregon—got a recent tour of the apartment, he said approvingly: "There are plenty of houses that aren't this big.")

My parents had lived in the apartment for almost twenty years at that point, so it was extremely comfortable. There were four televisions (even though there were only three people who ever lived there) and a vast library of books and videos.

And unlike friends of mine who had to move to neighborhoods that were still up and coming and still had plenty of safety concerns, like Fort Greene or Harlem, my parents lived in Brooklyn Heights, which was quite possibly the most beautiful neighborhood in the whole city. Their apartment building was on the same block with five different subway lines. You could get to Union Square in fifteen minutes, which is an impressive claim for any New York apartment to make.

And, finally, when you're paying nothing in rent and nothing in utilities and nothing in phone charges and nothing for cable and there's a refrigerator full of free food at your fingertips . . . well, you begin to wonder what's so great about living on your own, anyway?

Now I can only think a little wistfully back to the days when I didn't owe American Express any money. When I looked at my bank balance and it was comfortably over $700. When I didn't have to wait more than an hour to get home late at night. When I could turn on the television and watch *Curb Your Enthusiasm* on one of seven different HBO channels.

Of course, it wasn't all comfort. My father was a cranky sexagenarian, and I was a brash twenty-two-year-old. We fought a lot. Our fights were mostly about politics—which was something of a sport around our house—but it was occasionally about more serious things like forgetting to clean my beard shavings in the sink, or leaving empty tea cups in the den.

And weird issues (things that you would have thought were long since settled) manage to rear their heads too like, say, curfew.

I can't remember ever having a conversation about curfew when I was in high school (partly because I rarely went out), but it became a big concern now that I was an adult.

"You can't keep coming home as late as you did last night," my mother said to me one morning. "You woke your father up."

"Okay," I said, "how about I promise to be more quiet when I come in next time?"

She agreed to this at first, but after a few more late night entrances through the front door (sometimes having had a glass or two of whisky and doing a terrible job of keeping quiet), I was told again that as long as I was living under their roof, I had to respect their rules. No more stumbling in at two in the morning. We never settled on an exact time, but it had to be earlier.

This reached an embarrassing climax for me when I stayed late at a party in Williamsburg one night. When I realized it was well past two and I was too tipsy to go home, I curled up on a futon beside an old college flame and fell asleep. The next morning, I was woken up at six by the sound of my father's voice on my host's answering machine. "Uh, this is Ken Gross, I'm looking for my son . . ." the message began. When I rushed for the phone and assured my father that I was safe and on my way home, he was too angry to even speak. He hung up on me. For a few minutes, I fiddled with the answering machine in an attempt to erase his message, but I couldn't figure out how to do it without erasing all the other messages. (The host of the party later said to me: "Yeah, I got the weirdest message for you on my answering machine . . . none of us could figure it out.")

And your sex life takes on a monk-like dynamic when you live with your parents.

The very idea that you live at home sounds hopelessly pathetic and serves as an immediate turn-off to any girl who might have been interested in you. A girl can get away with living at home—a guy cannot.

The immediate image that is summoned up is a nearly insurmountable one to live down: bad provider.

If you can't even get some sort of apartment, how can you be expected to be any kind of decent husband? Or father?

You can bring up all the defenses you like; you can tell the girl that you don't get along well with roommates and that's the reason you've been living at home. You can tell her that you're a slave to your dream of becoming a writer, and writers don't make a lot of money. (Some girls might think that it's a "romantic" profession and that it's admirable that you're taking a chance—but these girls are exceedingly rare.) You can say that it's all temporary, and that you're looking for an apartment as you speak. You can say anything you like. And the girl might even be sympathetic. She might say something encouraging, and even agree to go out with you. But no matter how fervently she protests to the contrary, there is some deeply embedded gene that tells her that a guy who lives with his parents is a bad prospect.

For the better part of the year that I was living at home, I almost exclusively went out with girls that lived with their parents, too. This wasn't out of design, necessarily, but they were the only ones understanding enough to give me a chance.

None of these dates ever developed into big romances, however. This was mostly because they couldn't. Once you've got past the initial awkwardness of admitting you're still at home, and you've managed to charm the girl anyway into thinking you're funny enough and cute enough to fool around with, where do you take a girl when you're both living at home? My parents *never* went out, and I certainly wasn't about to bring a girl home to find my father in his pajamas sprawled out on the living room couch. If you're lucky, you feel her up in the cab ride to her house. That's about all you can expect.

But for six or seven months, anyway, I was fairly sanguine about the whole matter. Romance would come my way eventually, I reasoned. As would a full-time job. As would an apartment without roommates.

I might have become one of those extremely sad cases of a guy who finds himself still unemployed and still living in his mother's house at age forty if I hadn't met a friend from college named Craig Walzer at the White Horse Tavern one August evening.

"So how are things?" Craig said.

"Pretty good."

"Where are you working?"

"Oh," I said, "I don't have a full-time job. I've been temping a bit. And writing for *The Forward*—you know, an article or two a week."

Craig nodded. "That's cool. Are you dating anybody?"

"No," I said. "I've gone out on dates, but nobody steady. Not recently."

"Where are you living?"

"Brooklyn Heights."

Craig looked up.

"Isn't that where you grew up?" he said.

"Yeah."

"But you're not living at home, are you?"

"I am."

A mischievous smile crept across Craig's face. "Okay, *Costanza!*" he cried.

I'm sure Craig meant no harm. (I am, in fact, extremely grateful to him today for saying that.) And at the time I laughed loudly—if only to cover my embarrassment. But it was one of those very uncomfortable epiphanies about a life that has gone (if only slightly) off the tracks. "Oh, my God," I thought to myself. "I've become George Costanza!"

There was no escaping it. I had no job. I had no apartment. I had no girlfriend. How was I any different?

And I spent the rest of the evening under a cloud, trying to think of something I had going for me that George didn't have. The only thing that came to mind was that my parents were somewhat less difficult than Frank and Estelle Costanza, which is cold comfort.

On my way home, I stopped at an ATM and checked my balance. It was healthy in those days, and as I got on the subway, I began making calculations in my head. I could afford about $900 per month in rent for the next seven or eight months. And you could find a studio or a small one-bedroom for that kind of money. I would probably have to find some sort of permanent job by the end of eight months, but I could do that, couldn't I? I might not be able to find something in a nice neighborhood but, really, what did I care?

"I think I'm going to move out by September first," I told my mother the next morning at breakfast.

She looked up from her grapefruit, surprised.

We had talked as a family about the day I would move out on my own in somewhat vague terms, but nothing had been set at that point. And at that moment, I suspected for the very first time that my parents had written me off as the failed child who still needed a lot of retooling before he could be set loose in the world. The look on my mother's face was too surprised to mean anything else.

She smiled.

"Good," she said. "I'll help you."

I spent about two weeks perusing the classifieds and even went to the then-unknown web site craigslist. I visited apartments in Harlem and Fort Greene and Flatbush. One evening I took the subway out to Bay Ridge to look at a one-bedroom. The evening air was balmy, and as I walked along the row-houses of the neighborhood (I had never been to Bay Ridge before) and the Arab and red-sauce Italian restaurants of Third Avenue, my heart sang.

The apartment was bigger than I expected, and the rent was $865 per month. "I'll think about it," I told the two girls who were moving out.

But by the time I got home my mind was made up.

I called them up that night and said, "I'd really like the place if it's still available."

I moved out of my parents' house in September—a few weeks before starting a full-time job at *The Forward*.

House rules for living with fellow schlubs

Should the unthinkable happen and you are forced to live with other schlubs, it might be wise to spell out the rules in advance—that way no one will feel like the chump, living in an arrangement he wasn't expecting. So—

1) Cleaning

Pick a day of the week to be your designated cleaning day and split up the household chores. Or the neater of the two roommates could take greater pains not to give a shit. To maximize comfort, I'd advise the latter.

2) Common areas

If *The Big Lebowski* is on, that's what we're watching.

3) Dating

Whenever one of the roommates begins a relationship, your average schlub will seethe with jealousy. Particularly if the roommate uses his room for their assignation. The girlfriend should have the good grace to start bringing friends.

4) Food in the refrigerator

Hey, I didn't see your name on it . . .

5) Dishes in the sink

Avoid leaving dishes in the sink by drinking straight from the milk carton and eating directly from the Chex box.

6) Shopping for the apartment

Toilet paper must never be allowed to run out. Ever.

7) Pets

They should generally be avoided (schlubs do not make for great pet owners) but if you must have one, it should be the kind that can be fed once every six months and still be okay. Like a snake or a camel.

8) Noise levels

You should keep it down after 11 PM. How many times can you laugh at John Goodman smash that damn car up? (A lot, I know, but try to control yourself.)

9) Bills

You threw up on the rug, you have to pay the cleaning bill.

10) Parents coming for a visit

You're both better off just moving.

Chapter Four*

*What's Schlub Got To Do With It?

"Wouldn't this be a great world if insecurity and desperation made us more attractive? If *needy* were a turn-on?"

—Albert Brooks, *Broadcast News*

When I was about seventeen or eighteen years old, my father took me to dinner at Le Cirque with Abe Hirschfeld, the billionaire crackpot who later went to prison for trying to have his partner murdered. (At the time, my father was contemplating writing a biography about Hirschfeld.)

Hirschfeld greeted me with a grin.

"A handsome boy," he said to my father.

I smiled and thanked him.

Hirschfeld continued to look me over for a minute. I was dressed for a fancy dinner—sports jacket, loafers, and tie—but it's a difficult thing to escape one's essential schlubbiness, and Hirschfeld saw mine. My hair was overgrown. And my glasses were smudged. There must have been something about me that seemed to give off the whiff of a bookish intellectual who was a little too innocent of the world.

"He doesn't look like he does well with the girls, though," Hirschfeld pronounced. "I'll bet he's never had any girl, has he?"

I chuckled good-naturedly. (What else could I do?) And I consoled myself with the fact that I wasn't *quite* as green as Hirschfeld had assumed. But I would be lying if I didn't admit that, yes, I was woefully inexperienced at that age. And when you're at the end of your teenage years, a lack of sexual experience is an unremitting source of shame.

More than a source of shame—it's the predominant focus of an eighteen-year-old's thoughts and wishes.

In those days, I thought about sex on the subway. I thought about sex at the grocery store. I thought about it in the waiting room at the dentist's office, and I thought about it when passing a marginally good-looking woman on the street (and sometimes less than marginally good-looking). Heck, I thought about sex in synagogue on Yom Kippur. (Synagogue tended to bring out more sexual thoughts in me than most other settings. What else are you supposed to think about when trying to keep awake?)

But when I thought about sex, I mostly focused on the maddening, teeth-grinding injustice that I wasn't getting any!

The fact that very few girls were willing to date me (and the few who did go out with me rarely wanted to end the date on a kissing note) was a constant obsession. I absolutely couldn't figure women out, and it was endlessly frustrating.

Moreover, when you're that age (and when it's on your mind to such an extent), sex is the first and foremost topic of conversation with your friends. From the coolest to the schlubbiest, it's the one subject that can unite a room full of teenage males. And I had embarrassingly little to boast about.

To countenance the absence of real experiences, I exaggerated the hell out of those few encounters I did have. I described fairly innocent good night kisses as long make-out sessions. Actual make-out sessions were expanded to include toplessness on the girl's part. And so on. My pals never thought to challenge me on any of this—and I never challenged them on their stories, either. (Even though, in retrospect, some of their stories probably wouldn't have held up under inspection: One friend told me that he once got a 25 percent discount from a hooker in Amsterdam for being such a prodigious lover. I'm not so sure about that one.)

But Hirschfeld had looked at me for no more than sixty seconds and figured out the one thing that I was desperately trying to hide. It was almost as terrifying as it was humiliating. Throughout the subsequent dinner, I was burning with embarrassment. And as I stared into my dessert, there was only one thought endlessly drumming in my brain:

Was it really that obvious?

Of course, every guy feels a sense of disappointment with his sex life when he's a teenager. The average male sixteen-year-old just has far more testosterone than he will ever have opportunity to use—and I was no different.

But what made this even more unbearable for me in those years was the fact that I always believed I had the raw materials to become a great ladies' man.

First off, I fancied myself a writer, and a good writer should be able to come up with something witty or romantic or just plain intelligent to say, shouldn't he?

Plus, I was an actor who played a role in nearly every production that our school put on, and I liked to believe I was decent at it. Couldn't a good actor channel Marlon Brando—in his pre-orca days—if he needed to? How hard was it to pretend I had the confidence and fire of a Stanley Kowalski?

And even though I always presented myself as a joker, who didn't take life too seriously I was also—in my heart of hearts—a sappy romantic. Yes, I read Jane Austen novels and, yes, I loved them dearly. (No—I'm not gay.) I believed in things like gallantry and true love. And I held a torch for a number of the beautiful women I knew, hoping they would some day wake up and fall head over heels for me, too. "If only they knew the depths of my affection," I often mused a little wistfully. (I'm sure they probably would have run.)

Finally, I believed I had charm in my blood. My father never let me forget that when he was my age he was a lothario who had more dates than he could handle, and I felt it was my birthright that I should have inherited some of his prowess. (My father was decidedly *not* a schlub.) When I was a freshman in high school and hadn't even kissed a girl yet, I asked him if he had a girlfriend when he was my age. "Are you kidding? I was a probably a father by the time I was your age."

Throughout my youth, I heard of Casanova-like exploits. He told me about the Israeli models he dated; about the insane jealousy he stoked amongst his ex-girlfriends and ex-wife (he'd had one unsuccessful marriage and two daughters before meeting my mother); about the trail of women's underwear that he would find scattered around his old Queens apartment in the mornings, like a trail of breadcrumbs.

And even though most males treat their youth with some exaggeration, I'm pretty sure that my father was being candid. For one thing, I witnessed his charms, firsthand. Almost without trying, he would encounter a stern cashier, or a dour secretary and make some quip or joke that would melt the woman immediately. Well into his sixties, he would have decades-younger women flashing him big grins and winks and little sunbursts of appreciative laughter. (My father bristles when my mother and I tease him about this, but it's the honest truth.)

It was endlessly depressing that almost none of his seduction techniques rubbed off on me.

Not that I didn't know how to flirt. By the time I got to college, I was known as a cutup who could almost always get a laugh out of a girl. But I was a little too eager. I was a little too boastful (why I thought boasting was an attractive quality I'm still puzzled by). I was a little too attentive and enthusiastic to come off as anything other than desperate. (And desperation, as everyone knows, is fatal.) And, most importantly, I never mastered the subtle—but crucial—switch from being funny into being serious. When your hands begin circling over a woman's shoulders and you begin looking into her eyes, she can't think you're a complete clown.

I would make my fumbling moves, and have to endure the humiliating rebuke of watching the girl get up and move to a different chair. Or I would lose my courage, offer up a friendly, "Good night," and be furious with myself for days after.

And, like most schlubs, I had notoriously bad luck. Even after I had tasted my first few real successes in college, bad luck continued to haunt me.

I remember one summer evening after one of my first relationships went awry being invited to a friend's country house in upstate New York for a party. As the night wore on and the party took a late turn towards the intimate, I took a seat on the stairs with a drink in my hands and watched quietly as the various men and women (who were strangers only a few hours earlier) started dancing more slowly and looking at each other more longingly.

At this point, a raven-haired young lady with deep brown eyes and cat-rimmed glasses decided to take a seat one step down from me.

"So, how's it going?" she said.

"Fine."

"Some party, huh?"

"Some party."

She looked me over for a few seconds.

"You know," she said, "I'm Beverly's best friend."

Beverly was the relationship that had just ended. She was also the first girl I had the nerve to actually break up with.

In those days, as a rule, I didn't break up with girls. I figured it was only a matter of time before a girl broke up with me so my modus operandi was—in true coward's fashion—to simply wait out the clock. But Beverly was very kind and sweet, and actually seemed to genuinely care for me. This was extremely worrying.

I was afraid that she would fall in love before she got around to breaking up with me, so I felt I had no choice but to end things as quickly as possible. The subsequent break-up had, indeed, been unpleasant (they always are), but it could have been worse. We agreed to be friends after, and I felt that there was a solid chance we would be.

But when the raven-haired girl said she was Beverly's friend, I immediately tensed up and readied myself for an argument or an accusation. (It wouldn't have been the only argument of the party; an upstairs bedroom was, at that very moment, being occupied by a woman who was sobbing her eyes out.) However, there was something in the raven-haired girl's tone that didn't sound angry or confrontational. Instead, it was throaty and whispery. Like she was trying to seduce.

"I was really hoping to hate you," she said, leaning in towards me. "I'm *very* disappointed."

I have often wondered if she was giving me a line. But, if she was, it was one of the best lines I had ever heard. (I mean, it sounded straight out of a movie!) In two sentences she had flipped the conversation around entirely. And, I should add, this raven-haired girl wasn't just speaking flirtatiously—she was backing up her teasing, provocative voice with the full weight of her body: without a hint of fear or shame, she placed a hand on my leg, and stared unblinkingly into my eyes.

I couldn't believe my luck!

"I like you, too," I said. (In retrospect, I was stunned I could even get that much out.)

"You know we talked a lot about you," the raven-haired girl said.

"No, I didn't know that."

And as she talked—all the time in a low murmur that I had to lean in to hear, all the time gently stroking my leg—I was only think-ing one thing: "Don't fuck up." Because if my experience had taught me anything it was that when a woman puts her hand on your leg, it's pretty much a sealed deal. Sure, things could go wrong, but at that point, the girl has the requisite amount of attraction towards you. The only thing I was worried about was timing. She continued speaking in her whisper (I have long since forgotten what she said), and I just kept waiting for a real pause—something natural, some-thing unforced—and in that pause I would try to kiss her.

"There's something I want to do to you," she finally said.

I held my breath for a moment.

"Okay."

She grinned mischievously.

A moment later I felt a smack alongside my cheek.

She had hit me.

Hard.

It was, in fact, hard enough that my glasses spun off my nose and landed on the floor. And for a moment, I was too stunned to speak.

"I'm sorry," the raven-haired girl said, now on her feet. "I had to do that."

She walked away.

And having reflected on the incident at length, I think I should have been more suspicious. Nobody can be *that* bold. And we hadn't really spoken before that encounter on the stairs, so why should she have liked me as much as she claimed she did? (I honestly don't recall whether I said anything particularly funny or interesting that evening.) In retrospect, there were reasons to be more on guard. But either way, it seems like one of those emblematic hard luck stories that your average schlub has to endure.

As I continued to sit on the stairs, now in a complete daze, I could only think of the old Woody Allen movie, *Play It Again, Sam*, in which Woody lands a date with a nymphomaniac. The two of them wind up alone on the couch in her candle-lit apartment. The nympho is ranting about how uptight most women are and how uninhibited she is. Then she declares: "I believe in having sex as often, as freely, and as intensely as possible!"

Woody then makes a pass at her.

"What do you take me for?" she cries, shooing him away.

As he's walking home alone in the dark, Woody can only mutter to himself: "How did I misread those signs?"

Hey, I hear you, brother.

But despite the fact that the schlub has obvious problems as a dater, he also has one big advantage:

Hollywood is on his side.

True, the richest, the most popular, and the most recognized actors are always going to be the Brad Pitts and Tom Cruises of the world. They have an extremely comfortable perch at the top of the pecking order that (let's be honest) will probably never be traversed by the Garry Shandlings, Seth Rogens, and Woody Allens.

But these lower-order schlubs and nebbishes have not done bad for themselves.

The thing that was always interesting about nebbishes like Woody Allen was the fact that beneath his too-nice, too-smart, never-trying-to-offend exterior, he was a secret swinger who was much more adept with women than he let on. (Pauline Kael called him "a closet case of potency," which sounds like a fairly perfect description to me.) Woody might be able to rattle off opinions on Dostoevsky and Kierkegaard and talk about all sorts of weighty philosophical or literary issues, but the real object of his fascination was the female.

And at a certain point, all of these schlubs stopped trying to pretend they were Brad Pitt, and decided to revel in their Jewish nervousness (Allen and Shandling) or sloppiness (Rogen). They learned they could do pretty well.

True, schlubs and nebbishes are not for every taste. I remember a woman once telling me that she couldn't stand to watch Woody Allen movies because she could never take seriously the idea of a beautiful woman going out with him. And, to a certain extent, she's right. In his mid-sixties, Woody started looking somewhat ridiculous romancing hotties like Elizabeth Shue and Tea Leoni. (More than ridiculous. Even a fan and fellow traveler, like me, couldn't bear to watch Woody with Julia Roberts in *Everyone Says I Love You*.)

Likewise, *Knocked Up* was, in many ways, a schlub's fantasy. The pairing of Katherine Heigl and Seth Rogen is—if you're going to put it in polite terms—very unlikely.

But there is a subset of women who are attracted to schlubs. They like little pockets of imperfection. They like a *project*. Just as certain mentally unbalanced people enjoy finding rundown old houses and making them livable, certain women actually like finding rundown guys and whipping them into shape. And sometimes wit and intelligence can trump chiseled abs and liquid blue eyes and shirts from Giorgio Armani.

Of course, to learn this I had to go down numerous blind alleys.

Shortly after I began working at *The Forward*, that book, *The Guide to Picking Up Girls* by Gabe Fischbarg, came into the office.

"Why don't you hit the town with this guy?" my editor suggested.

I was intrigued.

"Your assignment is to get laid," another editor chimed in.

I chuckled.

Of course, the much better story was if I couldn't get laid—even after consulting an expert. (That was the funnier story, anyway.) But I decided to give it the old college try. And if the evening turned out to be a grand success, and I wound up going home with a hot model on my arm, well, I certainly wasn't about to complain.

So I studied the book learning terms like "wingman" which I had an only vague familiarity with from movies like *Swingers*, and tracked down Fischbarg who was extremely game to hit the town with me.

Before going out, he came to my house and picked out a wardrobe for me. My normal outfit was immediately discarded as way too casual, so he rummaged around in my closet and found out a pair of uncomfortably tight black trousers (pants are, apparently, way more important than I thought), painful wingtip shoes (I have flat feet, and change out of my New Balances only when I absolutely must), and a burgundy button-down shirt that made me feel heavy.

He also sent me to get a haircut and pick up some hair gel. (My mother was overjoyed and begged me to let her accompany me to the hairdresser. I reluctantly agreed.)

A few Fridays later, I went to Fischbarg's office wearing the costume he had picked out (having, earlier in the day, gotten the first shoeshine of my life) and we hit the town.

Naturally, I did not get laid.

We went to a Shabbat service at an Upper West Side synagogue which (to our disappointment) consisted mostly of couples and families rather than single women; we went to a Shabbat dinner for young Jews where we were seated next to other single guys;

we went to a bar and a couple of parties. I was as bold as could be expected; I approached numerous strange women and struck up conversations. When Fischbarg was flirting, I stood by his side as a loyal wingman, to take the pressure off. But I only got one number by the end of the evening—and the number was from a woman who thought I should write an article about her.

"That's only half a point," Fischbarg said.

In the coming months and years, I took other, more extreme, methods to finding a girl—all in the name of journalism, of course. When I was trying to bring myself out of a funk after one heart-breaking, shattered relationship, I went to an old world (sort of) Jewish matchmaker. The matchmaker sent me on a couple of dates that didn't go anywhere—and introduced me to a woman whom I had a brief fling with. But the interesting part of that experience was not so much in the woman I had the fling with, but in the fact that the matchmaker let me see what some of my dates who rejected me had said.

One woman was particularly cruel in categorizing my flaws: I apparently looked like a dork (hey, it's not my fault if I need glass-es); my hair was too bushy (well, the Jewfro is not for everyone, sweetie); and I was a little out of shape. (That was the comment that stung the most. My weight has always been a sensitive topic for me—see Chapter Eight—but when I met this girl I was slim-mer than I had been in years. I suddenly felt like all my efforts at dieting had been wasted.)

All of these experiences made fodder for articles of funny failure (which commenced my fitful career as the author of the HJW— "Hapless Jewish Writer"—column), but after I had spent a year or two working, dating wasn't quite the problem it had been when I was younger. I was beginning to feel comfortable in my schlubby skin.

Granted, I still had on average a respectable number of strike-outs, but I was doing much better with women.

I lost the fear and nervousness I once had when approaching women in bars or at parties. In a way, being a journalist paved the way for this. Journalism is a little like picking up girls: You have to approach (often hostile) strangers, and coax them to give you personal information about themselves that might not be in their interest to divulge. But if you are friendly and disarming, the subject will try to help you out. (In that sense, schlubs do have an advantage: We are a benign band of brothers. We are obviously harmless. It's also a great disadvantage.)

Goodnight kisses weren't the awkward, clumsy ordeals they once were. I began to be able to tell midway through the date how it was going and whether the evening would be kiss-worthy. (Thus, I learned when it was wise to split the check.) Plus, I learned to keep my expectations in check. Even though people in the movies tend to wind up in bed together on their first date, I found that this happens very rarely in real life. (Although it does from time to time.) I'm a big believer in the third-date kiss.

And when you've moved past adolescence (and actually had a few real experiences under your belt), rejection doesn't have the same sting it once had. You can shrug it off. There are—as your grandmother could have told you—plenty more fish in the sea.

And it paid off. One summer, I was juggling four or five different girls—and all of whom seemed genuinely interested in me. (An editor of mine dubbed them "The Maxettes.")

"You go on more dates than anyone I've ever met," said a friend of mine.

I turned a little red—but there was a part of me that was also beaming. My father would be proud.

I even began wading into the ever more murky territory of "relationships." My dating record no longer petered out after eight or nine weeks with a stilted, "We need to talk," conversation.

I had actual monogamous relationships with real life girlfriends. Women who promised to be faithful to me. Women whom I dated for months—years in some cases—and whose parents I met. Women who left toiletries in my bathroom. And these girls not only found me acceptable—they even loved me. (Or so they claimed.) I had only one bad instance where I told a woman, "I love you," and the sentiment was returned with the ever-lame: "I love you, too, but I'm not *in* love with you . . ." (It was also the first time I had ever told anyone I loved her.) But when I said those words for the second time to a different girl, I was overjoyed when it was returned with an, "I love you, too!"

My relationships even rose to the level where I engaged in the playful, giddy talk about "our" future (meaning, as I made a point of explicitly stating, marriage and children). It felt a little like playing house—I never was sure I was old enough or mature enough to really believe those conversations were real. But they felt wonderful.

As I'm sure you've read or heard before in some other form, in a weird, Zen-like irony, when you stop caring about scoring, your indifference makes you seem cooler and more attractive. Then you wind up scoring much more frequently. This was something that I sort of understood intellectually during my strikeout years but it didn't really sink in.

Try as I did, I just couldn't fake indifference.

You can rate your schlubbiness as a dater with this simple quiz.

The pick-up

1) **When trying to meet new people, you've found that the best place to meet a potential mate is:**
   a) A bar.
   b) A party.
   c) A book club or museum.
   d) The line at the soup kitchen.

2) **You find yourself in a bar and see three women sitting by themselves. You approach:**
   a) The attractive one who's probably out of your league.
   b) The one who is reasonably attractive and who you could see yourself going out with.
   c) The older woman who looks desperate and keeps making eyes at you from across the bar.
   d) The guys watching the ballgame.

3) **Having selected a stranger to chat up, you should try which of the following lines:**
   a) "So, what do you do for a living?"
   b) "So, why do you think Ben Stiller is a star?"
   c) "So, how do you think we should go forward in Iraq?"
   d) "I think I'm a little short for the check . . . can I borrow five bucks?"

The date

4) You've gotten the girl's number and you've called her to ask her out. You:

a) Ask if she wants coffee at a cute little dessert place in the East Village.

b) Invite her to dinner at an undiscovered, authentic Italian restaurant.

c) Get tickets to a Mozart concert at Lincoln Center followed by dinner at Jean Georges.

d) Ask her if she has a cute friend.

5) The check comes and you both reach for it.

a) You insist on picking it up.

b) You agree to split it.

c) You let her get it.

d) You tell her about your foolproof tactic of planting a roach in the dessert.

Back at her place

6) **Somehow, you've convinced her to take you back to her place. During a slightly awkward moment of silence you:**

a) Look her in the eye and try to kiss her.

b) Place your hand on her hand, bring it up to your mouth and give it a big smackeroo.

c) Grin and say, "You know, you've got an awfully kissable mouth," and wait for her reaction.*

d) Belch.

7) **You made a move. And the girl was receptive. As you're kissing her, you decide that you should say something romantic. You whisper:**

a) "I want you."

b) "I need you."

c) "I love you."

d) "I really shouldn't have had the soup—where's the can?"

---

* That line, by the way, is from F. Scott Fitzgerald and is remarkably effective if you can say it with a straight face.

The aftermath

8) **The next day you decide to:**
a) Not call.
b) Not call, but email.
c) Not call, but send flowers.
d) Call.

Answer key: If you answered "d" for three of these questions, you clearly have schlubby traits—but you're not an all-out schlub. At least not yet. If you answered "d" for between four and six questions, you're definitely a schlubby dater. Try not to reveal too much of your schlubby tendencies *yet* . . . after all, she'll find out soon enough. If you answered "d" to seven or more questions, you really need schlub rehab. Try to get a hold of me at the *New York Post*, and I will see what I can do for you.

Chapter Five*

*Growing Up Gross

"We are a family that has always been very
close in spirit."
—John Cheever, "Goodbye, My Brother"

A lot of my non-schlub readers might view this book as something of a curiosity, but not anything to be taken seriously. "Well," they might say, "this is all amusing. But I doubt it will have any impact on my life."

Don't be too sure.

Plenty of non-schlubs have minor schlubby traits. And they can come out in odd ways. You might one day wake up and discover that your child has gone full schlub—and you'll be at an utter loss to figure out how this happened.

Do you not take me seriously? Do you think it's impossible for non-schlubs to sire a schlub?

Well, if you want proof, you needn't look any further than your narrator.

Both Grosspère and Grossmère are snappily dressed, successful, and attractive, with no serious weight problems, and unnerving competence in life. (Of course, they could be lying.) I doubt anyone who has ever known them would ever associate them with the word "schlub."

But here I am.

How does such a thing happen, then? How is a schlub born to a pair of non-schlubs?

I think there are two main explanations. The first has to do with the fact that, as well as they tried to hide it, both of my parents had recessive schlub genes that refused to ever completely recede. (Everyone has a few schlub traits when you get right down to it.)

As a family, we decided that my mother wasn't ready for a cellular phone yet. Not that she would fail to master the basic dialing, listening, and speaking parts, but as my mother once declared: "If I get a cell phone, I'll die. It will ring while I'm crossing the street or something, I'll stop to pick it up and get hit by a bus."

No one could argue with her on that. There's a sort of spaciness to my mother; she can only focus on one or two different things at once. Some people cannot walk and chew gum. My mother cannot walk and talk on the phone.

This made her technologically phobic. And her lack of tech savvy wasn't confined to mobile phones. Bigger (and more dangerous) machines were so daunting that they were simply avoided all together.

Driving was a completely lost cause. She has a driver's license strictly for ID purposes, but never had the patience for the road. Her mind would drift to more interesting topics than the Mazda in front of her and the Mack truck behind her. She would only be jolted awake by a mistake—and mistakes are always stomach churning when you're in a car.

The last such mistake occurred when I was an infant and my sisters were teenagers. Obviously, I have little firsthand memory of the incident, but my father recalls getting a panicked phone call from my mother one afternoon:

"Come pick us up."

"Why?" my father asked. "What happened?"

With me and my sisters in the car, she had gone the wrong way down Broadway—one of the busiest, most frightening traffic arteries in the world. After driving for a few terrifying seconds into oncoming traffic, she managed to pull the car over to the curb and abandon it there.

That was the last time she drove—at least in New York. (This was one of her schlubby traits that I definitely inherited; I was once told by a driving instructor not to even bother taking the test. I would never pass. To this day I do not have a driver's license.)

My father seems to do a better job hiding his schlubbiness, but he's certainly had his haplessness and careless moments. He was also completely uninterested in technology. He had little knowledge of how to program a VCR or how to work the strange method of communication known as the internet. (He did, however, go out and buy himself a cell phone—but he still doesn't know how to get his messages.) Just as I asked my old college roommate for help when I wanted to double-space a document, my father has a half-dozen people he will call if something should go wrong with the VCR or the internet. (Shockingly enough, I am one of the people who knows more about these things than he does!)

But not knowing technology doesn't make you schlubby, I suppose. (A great deal of techies, after all, are schlubs.) And, in all fairness, I think it's more of a generational divide than a personality divide. It's more the fact that he makes such a half-assed effort to learn about these things:

"Who would *want* to know?" he has asked on more than one occasion.

He has a schlub's delusion that the world can be extremely simple. He'll walk into Circuit City and buy the sharpest, most up-to-date technology in the store—thinking that having the best product will end all of his problems then and there. And then he doesn't know how to work the thing.

I think this has something to do with another schlubby quality of his: a lack of concern for money.

For my father, life is more or less centered around lunch. And a shopping jaunt to Barney's. And a yearly trip to France or Italy. (Preferably all of the above.)

Few wealthy people live as richly as my father does—despite the inconvenient fact that he is not very wealthy. (Wealthier than I am, certainly, but that's not difficult.) For most of his life, he had a burning, pulsating desire to fuel the New York economy, single-handedly.

"You just want to spend us into the poorhouse," my mother would cry when they looked over their credit card bills and the monthly restaurant bill from our favorite Italian haunt, Queen. "Dog food! We're going to be old, living on welfare, and eating dog food!"

"Oh, come on . . ."

It was a familiar argument around our house (my mother has always been the practical one).

"Admit it," she once said in the middle of one such harangue, "you just want to fly to France, go up to the Eiffel Tower, and throw money off, don't you?"

This stopped my father in his tracks. And it stopped me, too. I pictured him standing on top of the Tower, gleefully flinging fistfuls of cash into the wind.

"Well," my father said. "Okay, yeah. Maybe I do. But, you have to admit, it would be really fun."

The second (and probably bigger) reason I grew up to become a schlub was because I was treated like a prince as a child—and if you're treated like a prince you either turn into Eliot Spitzer or Max Gross.*

My parents couldn't help treating me that way, you see.

I'm not sure what it is about the Jewish family that pins such wild hopes and expectations on their progeny, but it's very real. It's something that the most rational, sophisticated Jewish families cannot escape. Every Jewish mother believes that her son will one day cure cancer, and it leads parents to feel that their wunderkind is entitled to be treated very well in the meantime.

----

* There is a third possibility, but only if your son bears a striking resemblance to the schlubby milkman.

It's not solely Jews who treat their children like royalty, mind you. In that great tome of schlubbery, *Oblomov,* the country aristocrats dote over the eponymous young hero of the book with the zeal of cult members. Anything and everything that could possibly hurt young Oblomov is viewed with suspicion and fear. Anything that will increase Oblomov's happiness is given to the boy.

But I also believe that there is something attached to the Jewish DNA that makes us particularly susceptible towards overindulgence and over protectiveness. We have a genetic instinct to preserve our kiddies from the Cossacks raging outside. The modern day Cossack might no longer be a six-foot-five rapist—it might be something seemingly more innocuous like attending a New York City public school. But, nevertheless, the Cossack must be defeated. My parents could never bear the idea of exposing their son to such dangers. Private school it was, for me. Public school was one of the biggest threats used against me when I misbehaved or brought home a bad report card. "That's it!" they'd cry. "Public school!"

"I cannot believe that he has *never* attended a public school," my grandfather—a perennially practical man—once said to my mother.

The fact that every hour of my education had been bought and paid for, while a perfectly good public school education was there for the taking, stuck him as unfathomable. My parents basically shrugged him off in true Oblomov Family spirit, saying, "Thanks God he doesn't *have* to go to public school . . ."

Oh, if only St. Ann's had been the end of it . . .

There were so many trips to FAO Schwartz; there were so many fancy French meals; there were *so* many European vacations! (By the time I was nine I had already visited Versailles and the Luxemburg Gardens, stayed at castles in Ireland, and taunted the guard outside Buckingham Palace.)

I once dated a girl who told me that her father had never told her he loved her (well, not more than once or twice, anyway).

"How is that possible?" my father demanded. "Who doesn't tell his daughter that he loves her?"

"People express love in different ways," I said.

He dismissed this with a wave of his hand. Sheer nonsense, as far as he was concerned. Children had to be told constantly that they were loved.

And I certainly agree with him. Children should be regularly told that they are unconditionally loved. And they should be treated well. (Lord knows, it was a lot of fun being treated like a prince.) But, if I may borrow an unfortunate Republican phrase, this does create a culture of dependency.

I might have become a little more self-reliant had I not had an army of devoted baby-sitters throughout my youth. (Non-enthusiastic baby-sitters were not even considered.) The most enthusiastic of which was Susie Lynch, a copper-haired Irish woman who lived more than an hour away in the Bronx and who completely and totally bought in to the personality cult of Max.

I can only cringe when I think of this now, but when I was still a toddler and told Susie that I didn't want to walk up the stairs at our old Greenwich Village apartment building, she didn't seem to mind schlepping my carriage up two flights by herself. (This was too much for even my parents.)

And when my physical person was threatened, Susie was unafraid of shooting first and asking questions after.

There was a little girl in our building named Heather who bit me one afternoon as the two of us were playing.

Susie bit Heather in retaliation. (Now *that's* how you treat a prince.)

Of course, my status as a prince is only one side of the story of my youth (and a very sunny side, I might add). If I was the prince in the Gross house, my father and mother were the unquestioned monarchs. And history is replete with all sorts of stories of court dramas and palace coups. Screaming and yelling took place in the Gross court. As did nagging and haranguing. As did an extremely high number of fat jokes. (See Chapter Eight. I'd like to think that my parents were simply trying to protect my health. Of course, it wasn't as simple as that.)

And even though I was a prince, I was also partly a manservant. Errands and orders were barked at me, and I knew enough about where my bread was buttered to be pretty obedient. (There was also, as in every Jewish family, a Philip Rothian psychodrama. But, for everybody's sake, I'll save that for a different book.)

As many princes have learned throughout literature, the privileges of aristocracy come with a big price. I've often thought that I might have been a more focused, disciplined person if I had not had so many things made easy on me. I might have not been quite so schlubby.

One of the stories that my mother loves to tell is the one about the time we were invited by my mother's friend, Pucci Meyers, to stay at her house in the Hamptons when I was about twelve years old or so.

Pucci runs an extremely proper—almost Teutonic—household. (Her parents were Austrian Jews.) And before we left, we agreed to make the house as pretty as it was before we had arrived.

One morning my mother handed me a toilet brush and told me to clean the toilet.

"Oh," I said, staring at the brush. "You want me to clean the toilet."

"Yes."

I continued staring at the brush.

"Well . . ."

"What?" my mother asked.

"Nothing," I said. "It's just . . . isn't that what the flush is for? Doesn't that clean the toilet?"

My mother was speechless.

Chapter Six*

*Moving On Up

"Your position in the firm is not so unassailable."
—Franz Kafka, *The Metamorphosis*

One of the real problems that schlubs face is a tendency to grow a little too comfortable with their surroundings—even when surroundings are less than ideal.

Obviously, this is not always a bad quality. When life isn't going your way, it can be an excellent way of coping. It's important to recognize that bad things happen from time to time, and you shouldn't beat yourself up about circumstances beyond your control. Every so often it's necessary to throw up your hands and say: "So things aren't going exactly according to plan . . . So what? It could always be worse."

And if the schlub took the next logical step (i.e., set about trying to correct his less than ideal situation), this would be a healthy way to go through life.

But, from my own experiences, I've come to the opinion that it usually takes some kind of crisis before the schlub takes that next step. I have found myself making the "things could be a lot worse" argument a little too often.

"So, I'm working as a personal assistant at a tiny Jewish newspaper," I've told myself. "Is that so horrible? There are people who clean toilets for a living."

True, toilet cleaner is a worse job.

"So I live in Bay Ridge," I've protested. "So what? The neighborhood has charm and character. It might be an hour away from work, but is that the end of the world or something?"

No, it's not the end of the world. Just the end of Brooklyn.

"True, I haven't worked on my fiction in a while," I've admitted in moments of painful honesty, "but I've been really busy lately."

Indeed, there are busy patches in every life. Especially that of a single man on the prowl. It was to be expected that at that age, I would be sowing my wild oats. (Or at least trying to.) Even

F. Scott Fitzgerald went through dry spells when he wasn't writing every day.

"So what if my bank account is empty?" I've said after sobering visits to the ATM. "Is that a major catastrophe? I could be in debt, and I'm not."

No question: being in debt is worse than being broke.

"So I owe American Express a few grand," I've said a couple of months later after going out on a few too many dates. "Being a little bit in debt isn't like being addicted to crack. Or having a gambling problem. Hell, I owe money to American Express, not John Gotti."

No argument there. If you want to reach the bottom of life's pit, owing your credit card company a few thousand dollars isn't it. Tens of millions of Americans are in the same boat.

And, yes, these statements are all perfectly reasonable when standing on their own. But when taken together, they are a stark indictment against a lifestyle. I didn't realize that I had lulled myself into a rut.

I was a glorified secretary (and not even a very good secretary) for a small newspaper, writing articles on the side. I wasn't learning anything new about journalism, and I wasn't advancing my career. I was so broke that I had to *schnor* meals off my parents on the weekends. (I would call my father almost every Friday afternoon and say, "What are you guys doing tonight?" sounding, I'm sure, so Dickensian that he didn't have the heart to turn me away.)

And I was living in the far-off reaches of Brooklyn that none of my friends would dare to visit.

Certainly, I had a goal: I wanted to write books. But I hadn't worked on my novel in ages. I wasn't behaving the way a serious writer behaves if he ever wants to get published. I was just drifting.

And you don't want to drift into your thirties with your life in disarray. It was time to get my life in order, and—as in the rest of my life—I needed a swift kick in the breeches before I would wake up.

The kick came in the form of a heart-to-heart with an editor of mine one April afternoon, a week or two before the Passover holiday.

"Max," Wayne said, "do you have a few minutes?"

"Sure."

I sat down on the couch in his office.

"Let me ask you a question," he said, "what do you see in your future? What's the ideal sort of thing you'd like to be writing about?"

It's a weird sort of question to be asked by one of your bosses. Not that I didn't have some idea of what I wanted to be writing in the long run (books) or the sorts of things I wanted to be doing in journalism (longer, *New Yorker*-ish articles). But were you supposed to admit to your employer that you had bigger dreams than his office?

"Well," I said, "I suppose I'd like to write longer pieces."

"Have you pitched any ideas?"

"No," I said. In truth, I had sent a few ideas to the *New Yorker*. And I had a couple of encouraging rejections (they weren't encouraging enough to make me come up with something they would accept, but encouraging nonetheless).

"Well, let me ask you this," he said, "what do you see as your future here at *The Forward*? You don't want to be J. J.'s assistant forever."

And, for a moment, I wondered if this was a rare, glistening opportunity to get promoted.

"What I'd like to be is full-time writer," I said. "Maybe the features reporter?" (The features reporter, Lisa Keys, had decamped a couple of months earlier to the *New York Post*, and no one had been hired to take her place.)

Wayne stared at me for a few moments.

"I don't see that happening," he finally said.

I was caught off guard.

"I've been looking over the budget," Wayne said, "and we don't have the money for another reporter right now."

I had, in those days, fantasized about my "next move." Even though I was relatively comfortable in my position, I knew (even before Wayne had said anything) that it wasn't ideal. Not for the long run. I had tinkered with the idea of sending out resumes and clips to other newspapers. And I had even worked out a ploy for convincing the editors at *The Forward* to hire me full-time.

"Well, what about this," I said immediately launching into my ploy, "what about making me the calendar editor and giving me reporter duties as well?"

The Forward's calendar (which has since been discontinued) was something that was farmed out to freelancers for $300 per week. It was a time-consuming, but relatively easy job, and it didn't seem like such an impractical idea to give it to me along with reporter's duties.

"I don't think J. J. would go for it," Wayne said, matter-of-factly. "Frankly, Max, I don't think you have a future here at *The Forward*."

"Oh . . ."

I left Wayne's office looking pale.

And for the rest of the day I did my work in virtual silence. Rather than looking over a book or a magazine as I always did on the long subway ride back to Bay Ridge, I stared off into the crowds in silent contemplation. When I got home I called my mother (which only a schlub would do) and said trippingly:

"I think I was fired today."

Of course, I knew I hadn't been fired. Not technically. Not yet. But—as a somewhat clueless person who understood virtually nothing about the signals and cues that are made in business (or society at large, for that matter) and as an *extremely* paranoid person who believed that the world deliberated about me and my fate almost as much as I did—my thinking was that I had just been given my warning: I did not have long to last at *The Forward*.

And my parents—who are even more neurotic and paranoid than I am—concluded the exact same thing.

They panicked.

"Wayne was doing you a favor," my father said. "He was giving you a window. You better get your ass in gear and find something else right away."

"Yeah, I think you're right."

"Right away, Max," he repeated.

"Yeah."

"The clock is ticking."

And sitting in my apartment that night, I went slightly crazy with dread. I had long since reconciled myself to living paycheck to paycheck and my bank account had been bare for a long time. What was I going to do, exactly, if I couldn't find a job? I pictured myself pushing a shopping cart filled with my possessions into an alley. Or, less dramatically, I pictured the humiliation of having to return to my parents' apartment and my old room.

Both of these things I knew in my rational mind were farfetched. If worse came to worst, I could spend a few months temping. My parents would, I'm sure, loan me some money if I got desperate.

(Hell, they didn't want me back in their apartment any more than I did.) I had friends who were lawyers and bankers, and I could—if necessary—get some sort of administrative job for a few months until something better came along. (After all, a degree from an Ivy League college has to be good for *something*.)

But, nevertheless, I had fallen into worst-case-scenario mode.

"I *think* I was fired" had somehow translated to "I *was* fired" when I called a couple of close friends and told them about my predicament.

I had a trip scheduled for California the next week (my first vacation in ages) to visit my best friend. I canceled it. I wasn't about to let J. J. interview a replacement for my job while I was away. (Paranoia.) And I wasn't going to spend my time doddering around San Francisco when I should be spending it finding another job.

"Well, I understand," my best friend said. "I mean, it doesn't sound like you got fired, Max. But, yeah, that doesn't sound good. You should probably start looking around for something else. But you shouldn't panic."

It was way too late for that.

And underneath my veneer of panic, there was also a feeling of crushing betrayal towards my masters at *The Forward*. Granted, I was a pretty crappy personal assistant, but I thought I was a decent writer and reporter. I was always coming up with ideas and my weirder stories were the ones that were picked up in other publications or on web sites.

I couldn't fathom the fact that I wasn't valued enough to be promoted. Shouldn't my years of service count for something? And the budget excuse was a lie! A few months earlier they hired a handsome, easygoing young man (a year younger than me, with less experience) as a full-time reporter.

"Why him and not me?" I had asked myself at the time.

In retrospect, one of the more plausible explanations I could think of was the fact that they viewed me as a little too schlubby to take seriously. But I still cannot honestly say what it was about me that they never quite trusted. (I should also add in all fairness: that young hire turned out to be an excellent reporter.)

The next day, I got into the office early and began polishing my resume. I went through my old clips and began picking out the five or six best ones. And I began going through my in-box and looking for the email addresses of people who could possibly employ me (or who could pass my name along to someone who would employ me).

"I could get you a job right now, if you want," said my friend, Lisa, when I saw her the next night at a party.

"Really?" I said. "What kind of job is it?"

"It's part-time," said Lisa. "Basically, it's one or two days a week—you would come in and help close my section." (Newspaper speak for filling in captions and headlines and getting the paper ready to send off to the printers.)

"Would it pay enough to live on?"

Lisa shrugged. "Yeah, I think so," she said. "There are a number of freelancers and part-timers at the paper. I'm sure it's not bad."

Given the fact that my salary at *The Forward* was extremely bad, "not bad" sounded intriguing.

The next day I sent my resume and clips over to Lisa, and she arranged for an interview with Andy Wang, the deputy editor of *The Post*'s Home section.

But in the week leading up to the interview, there was an eerie atmosphere around *The Forward*—and it was not at all centered around my talk with Wayne.

I had heard a rumor that the copyeditor had been given two weeks' notice (which turned out to be true). And as I was getting ready to go home one night, the features editor called me into her cubicle. "I was canned," she told me to my utter shock. (The higher-ups had decided to throw out her section all together.) And my closest friend at the paper was told that he was going to be laid off in the coming weeks.

"This is like a Passover massacre," I said to my friend.

He snickered, softly.

Suddenly, my "firing" seemed much starker and more real. I wondered what the official firing would be like—and I dreaded it.

"Let's just hope this *Post* thing works out," I said to my mother on the phone.

The next week I put on a suit and tie and sat down for my interview at *The Post*.

Andy Wang, who interviewed me, was extremely casual in the twenty or thirty minutes we spent together. "Your clips look good," he said. "Basically, we need someone who can come in here and who can write a quick caption on deadline day; who can come up with something fast when we're closing." The salary for the one-day-per-week of work wasn't something I could live on, but Andy said that there would be writing assignments, and he would pay me for every article I wrote.

"I don't know if I can live on one day a week," I said, carefully.

"If you take the job, I can probably give you two days per week," Andy said. "Come in on Tuesdays as well as Fridays. Lisa says you're good, and if she says you're good I trust her."

I almost couldn't believe my good luck. As I walked back to *The Forward*'s office, I figured out that with two freelance articles per month, I would be earning more money than I currently was at *The Forward*. It seemed like a "duh" kind of moment. Of course I would take the job. "Thank God," my father said on the phone when he heard all that had transpired. Everyone else I spoke to seemed to agree that it would be foolish not to grab the chance while I could. "So you'll watch your pennies," said the girl I was seeing at the time when I told her how much the job would pay. "It won't be forever." (Clearly she didn't realize how bad the salary at *The Forward* was.)

A few days later I went into J. J.'s office.

"I have something to tell you," I said, "I was just offered a part-time job at *The Post*."

J. J. looked stunned.

"Really?" he said.

"Yes."

"Wow."

And for a few seconds, he was too surprised to say anything.

"Are you going to take it?"

"Well," I said, "you know how I feel about *The Forward*. I have real loyalty to this place. And I'd like to stay here. But it's going to be only two days a week, and it'll pay me almost what I'm making now."

J. J. considered that for a moment.

"Let me ask you a question," J. J. said, "what if I could give you a job as a full-time reporter? . . ."

My eyebrows shot up.

"With maybe a bump in salary," he added.

It was at that moment I realized something crucial:

I hadn't been fired.

I'm sure that at this point, most of my readers will assume that I'm not simply a schlub—I'm also mildly insane.

I would be lying if I didn't admit that, yes, I have my moments of neurosis and insecurity. I have the occasional flight of paranoia. There are gloomy hours (or days) when I somehow become convinced that life as I know it (and love it) is about to come to a fiery end.

But I think if there's a larger point to be taken from this episode, it's not that Max Gross is a nut (which, I suspect, most of my readers have already figured out by this point). It's that there's a need for the schlub to sometimes snap out of his schlubbiness; every once in a while, it pays to take stock of things and—if you're not exactly where you want to be in life—figure out how to get there.

J. J. wound up rescinding (sort of) his offer: the publisher told him that another reporter position wasn't in the budget—especially given the fact that they were shedding jobs left and right. And to a certain extent, I was glad. I didn't want to have to make a choice. Not that I wasn't excited about the next big thing in life, but I really enjoyed writing about nutty Jews like Mrs. Gottfried.

And I felt that J. J.'s gesture was enough: I wasn't completely unappreciated at my work. That was good to know.

Still, my position at *The Post* (even if it was part time) was a big leg up, which I'm sure I wouldn't have been able to pass on.

From secretary and sometimes-reporter, I was now working at one of the biggest papers in the country as a legitimate writer. The money was much better, and a couple of years later when Lisa left for an editorship at a Hearst magazine, I was offered her job. And with this step up, life began improving in other, subtle ways.

Working from home (which is what I did for about two years after leaving *The Forward*) really is a schlub's dream. If you've never done it, I strongly suggest you try. Getting up, getting into the shower, and settling down at your desk—less than five feet from your bed—is an extremely sweet way to live life.*

And my section of *The Post* was a pretty mellow place to work on the two days per week that I did have to show up at an office. As long as I arrived before noon on Tuesdays and Fridays, nobody seemed to care when I showed up. Suddenly, my mornings (which had always felt rushed and harried) felt calm and pleasant.

Now that my schedule was pared down considerably, I found that I was spending much more time working on my fiction. A year after I left *The Forward*, I wrote a novella. (Unpublished.) And I started getting ideas for others.

Plus, there was a notable improvement in the reaction I got out of women when they asked me what I did for a living.

In the old days—when I said, "I'm a reporter for *The Forward*," (I didn't feel a need to add "office manager")—I would always be met with the same question:

"What's *The Forward*?"

I couldn't blame these women, exactly. *The Forward* is, without a doubt, an exotic publication by twenty-something standards. But I would then have to fill them in on *The Forward*'s socialist, Yiddish, and English history. Which is fascinating, but becomes tiresome to repeat after the first two dozen times.

Nobody needed to be told what *The Post* was. Eyebrows would be raised. And I would find people paying much closer attention than they used to.

---

* Naturally, this poses a major danger to schlubs . . . you might allow yourself to get too comfortable at home and become slothful and withdrawn. And not a little bit weird, which is why a part-time job might be a good antidote: It gets you out of the house and forces you not to slip into a complete hermit's existence.

Just because you're a schlub, doesn't mean that you shouldn't have ambitions for your life. And it doesn't mean that you shouldn't pursue them. Like your narrator, this sometimes means getting a kick in the ass, but there have been some big success stories of schlubs who have made a name for themselves. Here are ten famous schlubs throughout history.

Job

The Bible is filled with stories of schlubs—from Esau selling his birth rite for a lousy bowl of stew, to Jonah having to be dragged back to Nineveh by a whale—but the guy who exemplifies the schlub best is Job. Job best embodies the schlub's "Why me?" complaint. The only thing he didn't get was bedbugs.

Ivan Goncharov

I have no proof to back me up on this, but as the author of one of the great anthems of schlubbiness, *Oblomov*, I think it's impossible that its creator could be anything less than a mega-schlub. He knows his subject too well to fake it.

Kaiser Wilhelm II

Well, if you fuck up your imperial throne so much that there's no imperial throne left after you've abdicated, yes, you're a bit of a schlub. Helping get your country on the losing side of a major war doesn't help. (Which is one of the reasons George W. Bush feels eerily schlubby.) Kaiser Wilhelm proved that you don't have to be a neurotic New York Jew to be an incredible schlub.

Herbert Hoover

When he came into office, the economy was looking great, and Hoover, no doubt, was looking forward to a drowsy four years filled with state dinners and speeches before the rotary clubs. He wasn't there for more than nine months before the Great Depression came crashing down—making him the Rodney Dangerfield of Presidents. But Hoover was, in fact, a somewhat decent guy. He was a strong believer in human rights and debt relief . . . he just wasn't prepared to deal with a crisis.

Fats Waller

Jazz pianist is usually way too cool a profession to ever include a schlub, but all you have to do is go to YouTube and watch this overfed musical genius sing, "Ain't Misbehavin'" and you'll see an unbridled schlub.

Golda Meir

She looked a little like your grandmother, a woman who seemed much more interested in talking to a reporter about family life than Arab-Israeli politics. But this adorable, bent-over little woman with a prominent nose also had the launch codes for Israel's nuclear arsenal. She wasn't just a schlub—she was a badass schlub!

Wallace Shawn

I feel a little bad for Wallace Shawn. When he is recognized, it is as the bumbling villain in the (overrated) movie *The Princess Bride*. Or, he's remembered as the high school teacher in (the far better) *Clueless*. But beneath his schlubby exterior is one of the most fecund, blooming minds you'll ever encounter. His movie *My Dinner with Andre* is one of my favorites—a brilliant duel of wits, between the distinguished director, Andre Gregory, and a balding, lispy imp named Wallace Shawn.

Mario Batali

The big lug looks like he wouldn't be out of place working in a video store or some other schlubby activity that doesn't require too much effort. But he also happens to be a genius when you put him in front of a stove. So he took on a profession which is extremely difficult for schlubs (working in a kitchen requires a lot of effort!) but few have succeeded as deliciously.

Chapter Seven*

*Sports and Manliness

"Grady Fuson, the A's soon to be former head of scouting, had taken a high school pitcher named Jeremy Bonderman. The kid had a 94-mile-per-hour fastball, a clean delivery, and a body that looked as if it had been created to wear a baseball uniform. He was, in short, precisely the kind of pitcher Billy [Beane] thought he had trained his scouting department to avoid."

—Michael Lewis, *Moneyball*

I am the only person I have ever known who has broken a bone playing wiffleball.

It's true. I was in the sixth or seventh grade, and we were playing wiffleball during gym class when I smacked the ball towards the back of the gym and took off towards first base.

Halfway there, I lost my balance, tripped, and landed on my ankle. I let out a howl and hobbled towards the bleachers. "I don't think I can put weight on it," I told the gym teacher. I limped down to the nurse, and came back to school the next day wearing a cast. I had broken my foot.

It was not the first serious injury of my young life (the year before I had fallen off my bike and broken my wrist), and it was not the last.

After my foot had been wrapped and I had been limping around with a cane (and, later, crutches) for two months, I tore several muscles in my neck because of the uneven way I was walking and the gargantuan backpack I took to school with me. For weeks, I was suffering from muscle spasms and migraine headaches. Another doctor recommended a neck brace, and there was a brief overlap when I was in both a cast and a brace. People who saw me back in those days assumed the worst, and used to ask if I had been in some kind of car crash.

No. It was wiffleball.

And my klutziness was not a problem that disappeared with the grace of age and maturity. During my first week of college, I became legendary around campus as "the guy who nearly managed to get himself killed on his freshman trip."

You see, Dartmouth offers its incoming students an outdoorsy trip where you go off in the woods for several days with your fellow freshmen and either hike or canoe or do something else that will accelerate the bonding process.

I chose to go mountain biking which was, in retrospect, a poor choice.

Not that I didn't enjoy biking. On the contrary, I spent plenty of time zipping through the city on my father's battered old Peugeot bicycle from the 1960s, and looking at the neighborhoods that my parents or friends would never dream of visiting. (It was pretty much the only exercise I ever took.) I spent weekend afternoons chugging over the Brooklyn Bridge and going up to Central Park, or through the Bowery, or along the East River. But—as most cyclists understand without having to be told—there is a vast field of difference between biking along Avenue B, and biking in the New Hampshire mountains.

I didn't realize that.

I think my parents sort of understood this. Before my trip, they decided to outfit me properly, and I was taken to our local bike shop and bought all the spandex a person could ever possibly use (*not* a pretty sight) in addition to a blue, brand new Mongoose bike that came with seven or eight different gears (something of a novelty as far as I was concerned) which, the salesman assured us, was the best model in the store.

I lasted a day and a half on my freshman trip.

The first day was murder. As we hit the trails, I was in the back of the group with a guy whose bike was missing a wheel. (Whom I kept begging to slow down.) I could feel my heart racing and my lungs collapsing, and I could only think to myself—over and over again—"What a mistake!"

"You should really switch out of first gear," the young man leading the trip told me.

I had no idea what he was talking about.

On the second day, we went up an extremely steep mountain,

and on our way down, my bike spun out of control and I woke up in a ditch by the side of the road, surrounded by some very terrified-looking cohorts. (This was in the days before the cell phone, and the two fastest bikers had to be dispatched to find help at the nearest place they could.) I was the first person on one of the Dartmouth trips to be taken to the hospital in years, and walking around campus the next week—with a massive bruise covering half of my face—I was instantly famous.

"Oh," people said to me, "*you're* the guy . . ."

But the accident-prone schlub doesn't even need a bicycle or a wiffleball to injure himself. I've done it while asleep. Not too long ago, I woke up with a pain in my foot, and when I went to the doctor a week or two later, he told me that I had a sprain as well as arthritis and a chipped bone. "Did you hurt your foot in some way? Were you, like, dancing, or running, or at the gym?" the doctor asked upon examining me.

"No," I said. "I just woke up."

But one shouldn't conclude that, just because I tend to injure easily, I (or other schlubs for that matter) have no interest in sports or other macho activities.

As a kid, I was an avid baseball, basketball, and (to a lesser extent) football fan, and I had the same dream all other boys had: one day becoming a starting pitcher for the New York Mets.

When I realized I wasn't talented enough to be a pitcher, I magnanimously decided to go for second baseman, instead. (It was the position my father played, and every boy wants to emulate his father.)

When I stunk at second base, I cheerfully went to the outfield.

And even though I was an odd kid who was also interested in less popular things like George Orwell books and Al Jolson records

(I did a fabulous Jolson impersonation), I knew all the same facts about baseball that the rest of the boys knew, like batting averages and on-base percentages. I had very definite opinions about starting pitchers and relievers. (Loved Dwight Gooden; hated Jesse Orosco.)

Perhaps the happiest moment of my young life was the evening of Game Six of the 1986 World Series when the Mets came from behind to pull off one of the most spectacular upset victories I had ever seen against the Boston Red Sox. I was watching the game in the apartment of a Yankees fan, and he could only laugh at how ridiculous I looked running around his apartment from room to room whooping and hollering in glee—not able to quite believe what I had just seen with my own eyes.

My joy and happiness was only eclipsed two nights later when my father surprised me with tickets to Game Seven—which was far and away the coolest thing that had ever happened to me.

And although I admit that, yes, I am a genuine klutz who perhaps has little business actually playing sports, my love for sports remained intact. I was a willing (if unexceptional) player, too: I was good enough to make my high school baseball team (which I admit was a relatively low bar), and one of the proudest, most gleaming moments of my youth was when I smacked a monstrous homerun against my math teacher in my senior year of high school during the faculty versus seniors softball game. (And, hey, I genuinely liked this math teacher.)

One ex-girlfriend who later broke up with me for—among other reasons—a feeling that I wasn't sufficiently "manly," couldn't quite believe that a nerd like me watched baseball. One spring evening, I sat on her futon and turned on the Yankee game, and she sat a few feet away, watching me watch the game.

"What?" I said.

"Nothing. It's just I never figured you for a sports fan." She licked her lips. "It's kind of hot."

I think part of this has to do with a long-standing Jewish obsession. Jews are constantly worried about the bad reputation we had back in Poland and Russia: We were written off as weak, bookish, defenseless. In the base, primal issues of the world (life, death, war, and defending yourself in a pogrom), we hopelessly sucked.

And for that reason, most Jews I know want to be very good at (or at least knowledgeable of) manly things. Even if we weren't blessed with natural ability, we made up for it with our enthusiasm. We might not all be Joe DiMaggio—but we can all be Howard Cosell.

Schlubs should, by and large, take a lesson from this. Even if you're embarrassingly bad at sports, a schlub should not emasculate himself. Every guy should care about the symbols of his virility—even schlubs.

Maybe that should read, "especially schlubs."

Besides, there are sports in which the schlub can display courage, discipline, and ability that don't require feats of strength or physical grace. Like, say, poker.

"Jews are obsessed with poker," the former professional poker player Avery Cardoza once told me. "Jews and Asians."

You can see Jewishness and schlubbiness (with a smattering of Asia) on full display if you turn on ESPN. The poker champs of today aren't the bluff Texans that once dominated the game—it's now slobs who have shuffled into the casino wearing shorts and shower shoes. (You can also add "professional poker player" to the list of schlub dream jobs.)

Poker has been an absolute boon to schlubs, tapping into our weird cross-section of skills.

A lot of schlubs, for example, are good at math and figuring out odds. (Even though I haven't cracked an algebra book in years, I always had a certain natural ability.) This is obviously an asset in poker.

You can be socially maladroit, and fill your poker-table banter with oddball observations and non sequiturs, and your opponent will think you're even trickier than you are. Giving your fellow poker players your thoughts on why Isaac Babel's short stories would make for a badass gangster picture will completely flummox them. They'll have no idea what to make of you.

And even though schlubs are definitely weird, that doesn't mean we can't detect behavioral patterns in others; we understand the way non-schlubs think. After all, it's schlubs who are the puzzle—not the normal people.

To give you an example of why poker is as much a schlub's game as it is a macho game, you need look no further than your humble narrator.

My first real experience of poker occurred in Israel just before the ESPN craze started. I was living with some Israelis and American ex-pats in the small desert town of Arad, and—for some crazy, unexplained reason—I did extremely well when I played with these guys. The stakes were extremely small: we played for only a few shekels at a time. On one extremely good night, I came away having won one hundred shekels (then about $25), which everyone thought was massive. I became known around my apartment building as the player to be reckoned with.

Thus, when I returned to America (a land of real poker players), I came back believing I was pretty good at the game. I even told my friends as much. Whenever the topic came up, I would inform whomever cared to hear it: "You know, I'm actually an excellent poker player."

Only one of my pals voiced any skepticism about this.

"You?" said my friend Alex. "But you can't hide anything!"

True. I have a problem hiding my emotions. (See Chapter Four, on dating.) But I had won on numerous occasions in Israel. What more evidence did Alex need?

"I don't know," he said, shaking his head. "I just can't see you doing that well at poker."

When a colleague of mine from *The Forward* invited me to a poker game with his friends, I eagerly accepted. It was a low-stakes game (most people bought in for about $20) and the ante was a single quarter. But on that first night, I managed to go through an entire stack of chips in only an hour, and then went through another almost right away. I had to stop myself from buying a third stack.

This was when my salary was barely keeping a roof over my head, and $40 was a devastating loss.

Walking home, I had the feeling of restless, impotent anger you always get when you just lost money. "Bad cards," I kept telling myself. "No luck. No luck at all!"

And then I realized something important: it wasn't poor cards or bad luck. The truth was, I was *not* an excellent poker player.

Come to think of it, I stunk!

And it shouldn't have come as a surprise that I could beat a band of Israelis; they stunk, too. If my pal Alex thought *I* couldn't hide any emotion, well, he clearly didn't know any Israelis. Whether it's something in the sand, or the sun, or the water (or the lack thereof), everything is an emotional issue for these desert people.

But poker is one of those sorts of things that I cared about getting good at. Not only was poker a game of men, it was also a game of writers. It was a game for Norman Mailer and David Mamet and Ernest Hemmingway. I felt I should improve (or at least not stink).

And unlike baseball, where if you don't have certain biological advantages (or growth hormones), you're a lost cause, you can improve your poker game through practice and study. Sure, the pros are in a different league than the amateurs. And if you were to pair me up with, say, Phil Ivey, there might be some shifts in the game, but over time it wouldn't be long before he had all my chips. But a schlub can't look at the champions of the game and not feel some measure of hope.

In those days, a friend of mine was working at a publishing house that specialized in gambling books. I asked her if I could get a poker lesson from her boss—a former card counter and professional poker player who had been banished from almost every casino in Las Vegas. He sounded perfect.

Avery Cardoza met me for lunch, and in about an hour, he improved my game pretty dramatically (see sidebar).

The next poker game I attended, I came out even. The one after that, I won.

Over time, I learned to be a good enough poker player that I found that other players (amateurs, all of them) were actually treating me with a great deal of respect around the poker table. I knew that I was no longer a crappy player after I went to a home game run by a fellow named John (I never found out his last name) who lived in Chinatown. It was about the right stakes for me (most people bought in for anywhere from $50 or $100), and the collection of Asians (most of whom worked in software or other mathematically based jobs) were endearingly schlubby. My first night there, I dropped $100 on a couple of bad hands. But when I went back a few weeks later, I won. Then I won again. Then I left one game with more than $300, which kept me going out to dinner for weeks. (I never lost at one of John's games after the first one.)

John was a pretty affable guy; he was an instructor at Hunter College. And he hosted games at least two or three times per week. The emails that came from John were always something along the lines of, "I know it's late notice, but I really got a hankering to play tonight . . ."

And then, one day, I stopped getting his emails.

For several weeks I waited in vain for an invitation, but it never came. And when I emailed him to ask if he was planning on hosting anything soon, he said, "Oh, I've been pretty busy lately." But his reply rang false. I wondered if I had done something or said something to offend somebody. (It has happened before that I didn't realize I had said something dunderheaded until it was too late.)

Then I figured it out: I was winning too much.

John wanted to keep the game loose, and I guess I took it too seriously. When he did finally invite me to a game a few weeks later and I started a winning streak, he looked at me and said, "Max, now don't tighten up on us!"

That was when I realized: I was *feared*—which is a very odd feeling for a schlub. We never know quite how to handle it. (It was also the last time John ever invited me to his poker game, despite the fact that I deliberately lost a few hands after that.)

And in my career as a poker player, I even managed to play with some of the heavyweights of the game. My editor at *The Post*, Andy Wang, was invited to a professional-poker-players-versus-the-media tournament at the W Hotel in Times Square, and he asked me if I wanted to go with him.

"It's not a cash game," Andy said, "but there'll be prizes for the winners."

"Sure," I said. "Sounds fun."

We walked from our office a block and a half west to the W with one of *The Post*'s ad guys, and as we were walking, Andy suddenly turned to me and said:

"Max, I think you're going to win the tournament today and write about it for *The Forward*."

"Huh? Why?"

"I don't know," Andy said. "It's just a feeling I have."

I have voiced similar feelings of confidence before a tournament. "I think today's my day," I've said. "I don't think there's anything that's going to stop me." This sort of pronouncement usually means very little. It's a way of psyching yourself up, I suppose. And sometimes it's honestly felt. We've all had days where we feel that the world is at our feet and there's very little that can stand in our way. (Even schlubs feel that way on occasion.) I've made that proclamation and won big—I've also made it and lost big, too. But I don't think I had ever had that feeling about another player.

"That'd be funny," I said.

And even though Andy was sure that I was going to win, I was not.

When we got to the W, a modern, glassy hotel off of Times Square, we went to an upstairs room where other journalists and poker players were standing around sipping cocktails. The event was sponsored by PokerStars.com, and they had convinced some poker top dogs to attend: Greg Raymer (aka "Fossilman"), the 2004 poker champ was there; as was Joe Hachem, the good-natured Australian who had won the World Series of Poker in 2005; and there was Isabelle Mercier, the skinny (and hot) French-Canadian female player who had won the World Poker Tour ladies championship; and, finally, there was Chris Moneymaker, the aptly named former accountant who entered and won a $40 online tournament and had gone on to the World Series of Poker where he won the whole shebang. In many ways, it was Moneymaker who became the poster boy for the ESPN generation: he had gotten to the Series through online poker, and he had beaten pros like Phil Ivey and Johnny Chan to win the tournament. The prize for that year's tournament had been a record $2.5 million. (It rose to a ridiculous $12 million in 2006, but probably won't be that high again for some time because in the interim Congress essentially outlawed online poker, diminishing the number of contestants.) Afterwards, Moneymaker was a celebrity; he dated *Playboy* models and wrote a book about poker. My best friend likes to call him the Bobby Fischer of poker. Which is a pretty good comparison, I suppose, minus the fact that Moneymaker isn't living in the South Pacific, with the paranoid conviction that a cabal of Jews is out to get him. But, yes, Moneymaker and Fischer both popularized their respective games.

And here I was—a schlub—who was about to play with these guys. No, Andy didn't know what he was talking about.

After various plugs were made for PokerStars.com, and after the crowd had become sufficiently lubricated with vodka tonics, we headed for the tables. I was seated with Raymer, who was cheerful. He was a heavyset guy telling charming stories about his wife during the cocktail hour, and who seemed like a kindred schlub. But when a dealer sat down and began dealing out cards, Raymer put on his trademark sunglasses, and I felt a shiver down my spine.

All I could whisper to myself was: "Oy . . ."

And at that point, my only hope was that I wouldn't be the first person knocked out of the tournament. No matter how good my cards looked when I picked them up, I vowed that I would not put all my money in the pot on the first hand. Under no circumstance. My hands trembled when I touched my cards. (Thankfully, my first hand stunk—I folded immediately.)

Raymer, on the other hand, couldn't have looked happier or more relaxed. (What did he care if he won or lost this tournament?) He took out a polished black stone and asked people at the table if they wanted to buy it for $80. (This is part of his poker personality; he's always using old artifacts—or "fossils"—as his card holders, and he's constantly offering to sell them to people at his table. Hence the nickname, "Fossilman.")

After a few hands, I was dealt a ten and a jack—both of clubs. A very good starting hand. I decided to play my first cards of the afternoon. I called the blinds, and Raymer stayed in, too.

The flop came with three more clubs—I had a flush.

Raymer made a bet, and I raised him.

Raymer looked me over. I had been sitting at the table for at least seven or eight hands, and I hadn't even called a blind yet. So he probably guessed that I was a conservative player. He looked at his cards and folded them.

The dealer pushed the middle-sized stack of chips towards me and I was ecstatic. "Well, that's enough," I thought. "I can go home now."

And suddenly, I was no longer trembling when I reached for my cards; I felt giddy. (I also had to keep reminding myself—for the love of God!—not to get arrogant. It could all end in a flash.)

Raymer didn't seem to notice my euphoria. He kept on playing. He doubled his chip stack—and then doubled it again a few hands later.

But I was playing extremely tight. And whenever Raymer came up against me, I had better cards. When we had another showdown, a few minutes later, Raymer dropped $200 in chips before folding.

And I was having one of those rare days of luck when, without trying, good cards come your way. I had flushes, straights, full houses. I don't think I won a single pot by bluffing. And even though Raymer was the chip leader at our table, I was the primary challenger.

Eventually, the two tables were combined. I took a seat near Moneymaker, who had also accumulated a tremendous stack of chips and, briefly, my nervousness returned. But, frankly, I was doing too well to be really all that fretful. And as we played for an hour, my chip stack (which was less than Moneymaker's) gradually grew.

More players got knocked out of the game, and after a while, Raymer went off to chat with reporters. The table had been whittled down to five players and what had been $750 in chips when I sat down was now well over $7,000. I had taken the lead.

I was dealt a pair of kings and bet heavily. Moneymaker studied his cards for a second and then said: "All in!"

It was definitely a painful moment for this little schlub. I looked at Moneymaker, looked at my chips, and took another look at my kings, to make sure they were still there. If I lost this one, I wouldn't survive the tournament. But, on the other hand, any poker player in the world would have told me to call. My heart was racing. But, then, suddenly I wasn't quite so worried. I had done well enough. If I got knocked out, it would be by the poker poster boy. You could do a lot worse.

"Sure," I said. "I'm all in, too."

Moneymaker flipped over an ace and a low, junky card. He didn't get another ace, and I was declared the winner.

Moneymaker stood up, shook my hand and went off to carouse with Raymer and the other journalists.

The president of PokerStars.com came rushing up to our table. He turned to me and said: "You knocked out a champion?"

"I knocked out Moneymaker," I said.

I was given the tournament's prize: a hardcover poker book and a brand new set of poker chips. Not thousands of dollars, it's true, but it came with great bragging rights. (And Moneymaker only enhanced my bragging rights: when I asked him to autograph my book he wrote, "Thanks for the lesson—Chris Moneymaker.")

I later wrote the experience up (as Andy predicted I would) for *The Forward* as a Hapless Jewish Writer column. (This was the column I had started after going out on the town with Gabe Fischbarg detailing some of my more schlubby and hapless encounters with the world at large.)

"You know," an editor at *The Forward* said, "you might not be so hapless anymore. You might have to think of something else to call this column."

A poker lesson from Avery Cardoza

Cardoza and I went out to a Japanese restaurant near Union Square, and he gave me the basics of how to become a not-too-terrible poker player.

We started out talking about five-card draw. "I'll bet you're betting on junk," he surmised, correctly. "What were you to do if you were dealt two sevens?"

"I would bet a quarter."

"No!" he exclaimed. "Two sevens is a bad hand. You should only stay in the pot if nobody raises."

Cardoza explained to me the wisdom of checking when you can, and the folly of raising unless you have to. He also gave me a number of books to read on the subject. (If any of my readers are contemplating a career or hobby as a poker player, the first book they should read is *Super System* by Doyle Brunson.)

But the most important thing Cardoza did was teach me how bad most hands are. There is real wisdom in folding most of the time (something a lot of first-timers don't grasp). Being that poker is, in the popular parlance, such a macho test of wills, this might sound counterintuitive. You want to feel that you have the guts to call every big hand.

And, yes, if you call every pot you might get a reputation as a man of huge guts. But you'll also get the reputation as an extremely shitty poker player.

"That's what separates good from bad poker players," said my father—who claims to be an excellent poker player "It's folding a great hand that you know is a losing one that makes for a real player. That's what takes the steel nerves."

When I thought about it later, that was some of the best advice I could have hoped for. I never had the heart to throw away three of a kind—even though I suspected my opponent had a straight.

So the mentality of the poker player should be to look at great hands and think of all the different ways that they can be beaten.

And, in a sense, this is what makes most schlubs formidable poker players. If you are really a self-deprecating person (and I think to be a proper schlub, you need to be), and if you're really skeptical about your poker-playing skills, you'll be very wary of betting on weak cards. Paradoxically, this will make you a much better player.

Just remember:

Two sevens is a really, really weak hand.

Chapter Eight*

*A Balanced Diet

"When a man is small, he loves and hates food with
a ferocity which soon dims."
—M.F.K. Fisher, *Serve It Forth*

I'm not sure that I've ever met a skinny schlub.

This isn't to say that they don't exist. Or that somehow they can't exist. There's no technical reason that a stumblebum can't wear a size small. Or have no strong feelings for pizza and hamburgers. I'm not saying it's not possible. And if you feel that you are such a schlub, I would gladly hear your story. But if you don't look like you can stand to lose at least ten pounds, I just don't believe you when you say you're a schlub.

By the same token, I don't think I've ever met a morbidly obese schlub, either. To get to such a gross level of fatness, you have to invest yourself in food to the exclusion of most other schlub traits. Fatness becomes your identity. I'm not sure it can coexist with schlubbiness.

Nevertheless, all the schlubs I know like to eat.

We retain a certain amount of baby fat that we simply cannot shake free of. Labels like "chunky" and "out of shape" follow us around our whole lives like a lost puppy who just won't get the message that we'd rather be left alone.

The puppy merely wags its tail.

My personal relationship with fattening foods began early; I was told that my first taste of pizza was—to borrow the George Hamilton movie title—love at first bite.

I had been eating solid foods for a few months when my father stopped by a pizza stand one afternoon. With his toddler in one arm, he purchased a slice with his other and blew and blew on the pizza until he was satisfied that his son's mouth wouldn't be burned.

I took a bite and chewed for a moment.

Without waiting to even swallow, I lunged for a second bite.

It was the start of a lifetime of incorrigible bad eating. Pizza is only one of the many life-shortening foods I ate rapturously as a youngster, and continue to eat to this day. I could give you a pretty exhaustive list of where to go for a decent hamburger anywhere in the city. I would be extremely content eating Chinese food every day for the rest of my life. And what about hot dogs! Oh, I used to love hot dogs . . .

When I was three years old, my mother was working as an editor at the *Daily News* magazine, and when they needed a cute kid to pose on the cover under the headline: "It's great to be with a wiener," I was tapped for the assignment.

I showed up with my mother at the photo studio in a Yankees uniform and was given a hot dog to pose with. After some pictures were snapped, I was allowed to eat said hot dog. I was given another. Then another . . .

One of the first childhood memories was the misery I felt in the back of the cab on the ride home. (This did not dissuade me, however, from asking for a hot dog later that night.)

Weight was a Gross family obsession for several generations— on both sides of the family. My mother was an enthusiastic eater as a girl, who would sneak into the family fridge for a sliver of cake that—in her retelling—would always expand into three or four, full blown slices. This would cause her such guilt that she would throw the rest of the cake away. (Thus pleasure and guilt became familiar feelings when it came to food.)

Likewise, my father was a chubby kid whom his brothers nicknamed (with the kind of cruelty only brothers are capable of): "El Gordo."

Inevitably, then, I was expected to weather a certain amount of hazing as a kid—not at the hands of my sisters (who were always protective of me) or schoolmates—no, it was my mother and father who didn't feel any restraint in talking about my weight.

And, yes, I heard a lot of fat jokes. Or sly hints that I wasn't keeping on my diet.

"Are you saying I'm fat?" I would say, haughtily.

"Well, I'm not saying you're skinny," my dad would reply with maddening glibness that would send me storming into my room in an uncontrollable huff. I would not speak to him (or anyone else) for hours.

It's a difficult thing to be a child teetering on fatness in a society that embraces junk food so fully. I couldn't understand why other children were given Oreos and Chips Ahoy! with their lunch, and all I got was a lousy orange. Any appeals I made to try to get more junk food in our refrigerator went unheeded.

However, this doesn't mean that my parents were not above using food as the ultimate bribe.

Whenever my mother needed a chaperone to go antiquing, or to go to a museum, I was promised a piece of chocolate or marzipan.

On our first family vacation to Europe when I was seven or eight years old, my mother lured me around Parisian art galleries and clothing stores with the promise of another piece of chocolate, like I was a trained dog.

"We just have to go to Bon Marché," my mother would say. "You can have two more pieces of chocolate if we go."

Who was I to complain? I would keep my head buried in a comic book and happily eat whatever my mother was good enough to give me while she tried on outfit after outfit.

My diet was complicated by the fact that I was an extremely finicky eater, who flat out refused to eat most foods.

I didn't care for salad—so I never ate it. And by "never," I mean never. If my parents were having salad for lunch or dinner I would ask: "Well, what can *I* eat?" Something else would have to be prepared for me. If salad was being served at someone else's house, I would rearrange a few leaves of lettuce around on my plate, but never actually put a tomato or a cucumber in my mouth. I'm not quite sure what I objected to—its coldness, its crunchiness, the vinegar in the dressing—but whatever it was, I was having none of it.

Other kinds of salad—egg salad or chicken salad—were not immune; I hated them, too. (I think it had something to do with the disgust I felt towards mayonnaise.)

Up until I was in my twenties, I never tried a leaf of spinach or a branch of cauliflower, or a beet, or a radish, or a stalk of celery that I didn't absolutely have to.

And fish was a total lost cause. Most seafood (with the exception of shrimp and lobster) I hated and refused to try—but I had a real aversion to tuna fish. In the case of tuna, I not only refused to eat the fish, I refused to be consigned to a table where it was being served. The very sight or smell of it would cause me to gag. If my parents were eating it, I would retreat to my room. Or, when I got a little older, I would leave the house with the expectation that there would be no evidence of their meal by the time I returned. (It remains the food I still have the worst aversion to and the only food I don't mind telling a host that I will, under no circumstances, place in my mouth.)

My hatred of tuna was so extreme, in fact, that it drowned out my passion for the foods I loved.

On one of our European vacations, my father told me about the famous restaurant, La Tour d'Argent, which, he said, was the greatest duck restaurant in the world—and duck was my favorite food.

"Well, let's go!" I cried. "What are we waiting for?"

"No, no," he replied. "It'll be at least a hundred bucks per person, and we've already had one really expensive meal . . ."

Well, I was not about to let that be the end of it!

I began a week long campaign of appeals to get us to the restaurant. "So," I would say. "Lovely day out, isn't it? It just makes you want to end it with a nice meal, right? Maybe we should go to Tour d'Argent tonight?"

I'm sure that not all of my entreaties were quite that lame and flat-footed.

My father persistently said no, and I persistently begged. But as our trip winded down, it was looking increasingly unlikely that I would ever see Tour d'Argent. (Well, at least not that trip.)

On the third- or fourth-to-last night of the trip my father and I were playing chess in our hotel room, as we did on all our European vacations (I was too young to go out at night, and my parents were too old). Through some sort of freak run of luck, I managed to beat him three games in a row (something that never happens), and I have a certain tendency (I'm not sure if it's schlubby or not) to get a little boastful when I win at something.

"So," I said, "not *too* good, are we?"

My father just stared at the chessboard, quietly.

"Want to put a little bet on the next game?" I said. "Maybe twenty bucks?" (Twenty bucks was two weeks allowance.) "Maybe fifty?"

I was getting very cocky.

"No," he said, "I'll tell you what. I'll play you for Tour d'Argent. But if you lose, you have to eat a tuna fish sandwich."

I was taken aback, completely!

"Wait a minute," I said. "Wait just a minute . . ." (My father seemed quite content with himself that he had come up with such a diabolical bet.)

"I can't eat a tuna fish sandwich . . ."

"Well, then you can't take the bet."

I looked at my mother for help.

"I'll do anything," I said, "*anything* else. I will streak the Champs Élysées naked. But I can't eat a tuna sandwich."

"Sorry," my father said. "It's a literary bet. It's either the best meal of your life or the worst."

Nearly an hour of begging and pleading did nothing to soften his resolve. Any offer I made was met with a shrug. And in the end, my hatred of tuna outweighed my love of duck. I couldn't take the bet.

Indeed, I was a child of ferocious feelings about food. But I think most schlubs are pretty similar. While schlubs are certainly coarse and sloppy—with trace elements of laziness thrown in for good measure—many of us are also hedonists, who feel that life is to be enjoyed. Certainly good food is to be enjoyed. Bad food is to be despised.

There are plenty of schlubs I know who are epicureans, and I think I became one myself. My pickiness didn't really go away until I was in college, but when it went away it never really returned.

I spent my junior year in Europe, and one evening my friend and future roommate, Dave (the same former roommate I discussed in Chapter Three) invited me to a Middle Eastern restaurant in London where he took the liberty of ordering a handful of weird dishes I had never tasted before and would have never ordered if I had been alone.

He requested sautéed chicken livers with onion, hummus,

babaganouj (this was at a time when no one had heard of babagan-ouj), grape leaves stuffed with rice and lamb and tabouli salad—as well as two or three other delicacies that I can no longer remember.

"Baba-what?" I said after the waiter had taken our order.

"Babaganouj. It's like mashed eggplant."

Well, I liked eggplant parmesan. No reason I couldn't like mashed eggplant, I suppose. But I was extremely hesitant—almost fearful. Chicken livers? It sounded revolting. Like the kind of thing generations of children pleaded with their parents to avoid. Being that I was nineteen and not so removed from childhood, I was worried. (It would, I assumed, not be very different from chopped liver, something I assiduously avoided up until that point.) And I wondered whether I should call the waiter back and order some-thing simple—like grilled chicken—and take my chances that Dave would be insulted.

But then something dawned on me . . .

"Why the hell not?"

What was the worst that could happen? I don't like it. Well, so what? There would surely be others meals in the future.

And so when the waiter set down a small plate of chicken liv-ers, I gamely picked up a fork, cut off a small fragment, and put it in my mouth.

The liver was velvety and rich and—at that moment—one of the most exciting things I had ever tasted.

"My God!" I said, in genuine shock, "this is delicious!"

"You see?" Dave said.

"I can't believe it!"

I next went to the grape leaves. Then the hummus. Then the babaganouj. And as we feasted in the little London café on George Street off of Edgeware Road (named Abu Ali), I was enraptured.

Having before and since dined at many two or three star restaurants, I still insist that it was one of the greatest meals of my life. We sat back and talked—another friend was also there, and we cheerfully waded into one of those great college bull sessions—and I felt that something fundamental had changed from the time I sat down until the time I got up.

I had, in one meal, turned from a picky eater into an adventurous one.

Are you skeptical? Well, you might be right to be. Most transformations are more subtle than that. And, yes, to a certain extent I had been poised for a change for a while. Now that I was outside of my parents' house, I felt a certain responsibility to watch what I ate and not blow up to a complete beach ball. Food wasn't quite as important to me as girls, and I knew that very few mentally stable girls were attracted to fatness. So, yes, I was beginning to broaden my horizons a bit. When I was on line at the dining hall, I felt obliged to take some steamed broccoli alongside my mashed potatoes. And I found that, no, vegetables weren't as bad as I remembered them. Fruit was an acceptable—even a welcome—form of dessert.

But this came with huge reluctance. I intellectually understood that everyone needed a balanced diet. When I put on my philosopher's cap, I even knew that if my wish should ever come true and I should all of a sudden wake up one morning with the metabolism of Takeru Kobayashi*, I would soon grow weary of eating Peking Duck and Doritos. But that was all academic. When I was being really honest with myself, I secretly wished for

---

* Takeru Kobayashi, in case you were wondering, is the 165-pound Japanese competitive eater who in 2006 set the world record for eating 53½ franks in twelve minutes at Nathan's July Fourth hot-dog-eating contest.

a life dedicated to junk.

But with one meal, my assumptions really did change quite profoundly. Not that anyone in his or her right mind could believe that livers fried in onions is salubrious in some way. No, not at all. It was at least as bad for your health as a sausage-laden pizza. But it wasn't junk food. It wasn't comfortable or familiar. It was something different.

Ironic as it might seem now, you could even say that Abu Ali was part of the reason that I decamped to Israel after college. There was something in the taste of the Middle East that appealed to me. This was, after all, during the 1990s when few people had ever heard of Osama bin Laden, and when the Israelis and Palestinians were engaged in the peace process. (Or seemingly engaged, anyway.) When I was making up my mind at the close of college on what to do with my life, it was either the Peace Corps in Morocco, or the Arad artist's project in Israel. The Israel option seemed the safer, easier bet.

Naturally, only one month before I got to Israel in 2000, the Second Intifada broke out in all its horrible agony. (This might also say something about my luck as a schlub.) So if you'd like to be flippant, you could say that my stomach led me into a war zone.

Bloodied, but unbowed, my stomach returned to New York at the end of 2001, determined to learn something about food.

Every week I would troll through *Time Out*, or Eric Asimov's cheap eats column in *The Times*, or read the invaluable Robert Sietsema in *The Village Voice* and make long (and often lonely) treks out to the far reaches of Brooklyn if I heard that there was an interesting seafood restaurant. (My feelings about fish—tuna excepted—changed drastically.) And I was constantly talking about food with my godfather, who is the food writer and former radio show host, Arthur Schwartz.

When I moved to *The Post*, I found in my editor, Andy, another kindred, die-in-the-wilderness foodie, and we often went on pilgrimages together to the clam shacks in Sheepshead Bay or Chinese banquet halls in Sunset Park or Flushing.

"You know what I'd like to write about?" I said to friends. "Food. I think I'd be good at it."

Many agreed.

After I left *The Forward*, my colleague Daniel Treiman also left and decided to start his own Brooklyn-focused magazine called, appropriately enough, *The Brooklynite*.

"How'd you like to be the food writer?" he asked me.

"Are you kidding?"

I spent the next year shuffling off to Caribbean restaurants in Fort Greene to rate the bluefish, or Sicilian snack restaurants in Carroll Gardens to see how good the arancini was. (If you've never had arancini, it's an enormously unhealthy delight—a deep-fried ball of rice with meat packed in the center.) The job paid a pittance—I spent far more on food than I ever recouped from the handful of articles and reviews I wrote—but I could tell people that in addition to being a freelancer for *The Post*, I was also "food writer for *The Brooklynite* magazine." It bestowed on me a certain coolness.

Sadly, *The Brooklynite* never became a weekly—or even a monthly. The second issue didn't raise the kind of revenue that Daniel was hoping for and he reluctantly told all of his contributors that the third issue was going to be published online.

Daniel—who is a sanguine person, anyway—took all of this rather calmly. I suspect he always knew that starting a successful magazine is a long shot. ("Well, it'll be cheaper than grad school," he liked to say.) But I was much less passive about the end of my career as a food writer. And I was no longer satisfied with making long trips to the far reaches of the city to try the weirdest of foods. No, I wanted to try much, much more. (Moderation isn't really a schlub trait.)

It seemed like the right time to be a food writer.

"I think I'm going to start a blog," I told my mother. "A food blog. I've even got a name for it: 'The fussy fresser.'"

She laughed. "Oh, that's good!"

It was an idea I had been toying with since *The Brooklynite* shut down.

It would seem like blogger would be yet another profession tailor-made for the schlub (it goes at the schlub's own pace and allows for the sort of impressionistic ruminations we're good at) but in a rare rebuke to my inherent schlubbiness, I wasn't completely sold on the idea. It would have required a lesson in mastering the computer—something I never had much interest in. And, in all honesty, I generally don't care for blogs (except Andrew Sullivan and Curbed). They're a little too shallow.

But when I brought up the idea to a friend of mine who was an editor at a new online Jewish magazine called *Jewcy* he had an intriguing proposal.

"You should do it for us," he said. "And then you'll get paid for it."

"Well, maybe . . ."

He emailed me a couple of days later to say that his boss thought it was a terrific idea. And that all I had to do was write up a few sample story pitches. It was all very exciting.

My career as a food critic came to an abrupt end one evening as I was preparing for a dinner party at my apartment.

Slicing potatoes, the knife slipped and I wound up in a nearby emergency room with six or seven stitches on my left middle finger. "Go to your doctor sometime next week," said the attending physician when she had finished sewing up my finger. "He can take the stitches out."

It was time for a check-up, anyway, so I called my doctor and made an appointment for a week or so later. He dutifully removed my stitches, drew blood and put me on the scale.

The scale was sobering.

I hadn't weighed myself for several months and even though I knew the results wouldn't be good, I hadn't figured on being twenty-three pounds heavier than the last time I checked. ("We'll subtract five pounds," said the nurse who could see the crestfallen look on my face. "You're not fully undressed.") And I went home in a state of complete fury. How did I let myself go so completely? How do you let yourself gain twenty pounds without taking a step back? No wonder I hadn't had a date in months!

But when I returned to my doctor's office a week later to get the results of the blood test, the news was far more grim.

"You're going to give yourself gout!" my doctor nearly shouted at me. "What have you been eating? Your uric acid levels are through the roof! The last time I checked your levels were elevated, and I told you to cut back. But now you've given yourself a completely fatty liver! This comes from eating purine-rich foods—things like cheeses, liver, shellfish . . . you've got what they call 'The King's Disease.' It's from eating too much rich food!"

"Oh . . ."

"This is really serious!"

"Oh."

Then he told me that my cholesterol was abysmal. It had jumped significantly since my last check-up three years earlier. This was always worrisome; there had been a long history of heart disease in the Gross family.

"Are you on any medication?" he asked.

"No."

"Well, you should be," he said. "We'll get you on something."

"Wait a minute," I said, my eyes now widening and feeling the first wave of panic. "Medication? Really? Isn't there anything else I could do?"

He looked up at me for a moment. "Yes," he said, "you can have a lifestyle change. But you will really have to change. Chicken instead of beef. Cottage cheese instead of cream cheese. Margarine instead of butter. Yogurt instead of ice cream. No liver. No shrimp. No lobster."

I nodded solemnly.

"Okay," he said, picking up my file and writing as he haltingly spoke. "Patient is making lifestyle change."

I left my doctor's office completely pale. I walked all the way back to my office stunned and terrified. "This is what happens when you don't take care of yourself!" I kept saying. And it is an important lesson for schlubs to learn. Food seems like such a relatively harmless vice, which is why so many schlubs lull themselves into chunkiness.

But now I was scared—and fear is a great motivator.

"I won't be able to order bad things for lunch any more," I told Andy, who had infuriatingly low cholesterol, even though he ate as horribly as I did.

Andy grinned, unwilling to quite believe me.

"I'm serious," I said. "No more. The party's over."

Andy had good reason to be doubtful. We were partners in

crime, as far as food was concerned. We were constantly ordering
kung pao chicken from the Chinese restaurant around the corner,
or Cuban sandwiches, or tacos for lunch.

"Well," he said, "we'll see how long that lasts . . ."

But when I got home that night, I went into the refrigerator
and threw away the Milano and Oreo cookies. No more desserts, I
decided. Or, at the very minimum, desserts only only two or three
times per week—not after every meal. Certainly no cookies in the
house. No more French fries. No more red meat—maybe once a
month, but no more than that. (I'll allow myself red meat once a
week now.) I had just turned twenty-eight years old, and there was
no way that I was going on cholesterol medication! I would not allow myself to sink that low that fast. I would be a changed man!

And, indeed, I did become a changed man. More or less.

I no longer went out to eat or brought in takeout for my dinner
but fixed a little pasta or a couple of fifty-calorie hot dogs. I filled
my refrigerator with pounds of blueberries, strawberries, raspber-
ries, cherries, and grapes and ate them as a snack (with pretzels). I
stopped going to the candy machine in my office, and began eating salad for lunch at least two times per week. On the occasions
when Andy would talk me into Chinese food, I would just get
some steamed dumplings or cold noodles or something steamed
and relatively not bad for you.

And for a while I started to get kind of haughty about fatty
foods. I would see fat people on the subway or the bus and in-
wardly shake my head and feel sorry for them. "How could they
show so little self-control?"

Within three months I had dropped more than twenty
pounds.

My pants started sagging—so much so that I was forced to go

shopping for a whole new wardrobe. (My mother was thrilled.) And shirts which had been too tight now suddenly fit like I had bought them yesterday.

And there was a big side benefit to becoming a slimmer man: I started getting dates again. I would walk past women in the street and see their eyes darting over me.

"She was checking you out!" my friend Noah would say.

One night, an attractive bartender even picked me up—which was a first.

"What are you reading?" she said when I had stopped by her little tavern with a book about diners that I was studying for a story I was writing.

"Oh, nothing much," I said.

I had met flirty barmaids before, and figured that her attention (as welcome as it was) wasn't particularly serious, but she took my number and, indeed, called me a few weeks later. I was so surprised when she called that when she proposed dinner, I assumed it was for business purposes. She was a budding photographer and I figured she wanted me to introduce her to photo editors or other photographers. "You know," I said, "I could bring one of my photographer friends and his wife along . . ."

"Okay . . ." she replied, with a touch of surprise in her voice.

I realized immediately how stupid that sounded. (But as boneheaded as that was, it didn't stop her from giving me a chance and we wound up going out for a few pleasant months.)

And there were other women whom I met who greeted me with grins and happy smiles and always seemed to be suggesting we go out to dinner or drinks.

"This was the best thing that could have happened to me," I told Noah.

Naturally, the moment I got a steady girlfriend, I stopped being as vigilant. I gained back just under half of the weight I had lost. But my new jeans still fit (way better than the old ones). I still avoided gamey meats as well as liver and shellfish. And after I saw some fleshy-looking photos of myself, I started getting back on track and dropped some of the weight I had put back on.

This is key for schlubs: There must be a constant vigilance. We might have to accept the fact that we will never be skinny—but out-and-out fatness is fatal.

Sadly, food critic is one of those jobs that schlubs with a poor metabolism should avoid.

Diet tips for schlubs:

So you've had the horrible (but necessary) meeting with your doctor. "Lose weight or die," he has told you. Well, none of us like to do it, but here are some foolproof ways that you can get your weight under control:

1) Stop making your restaurant reservations under the name "F. Bruni." The resulting shitty service will make you wonder what was so great about eating out in the first place.

2) Start eating a stick of celery before every meal. Hatred of said vegetable should only instill in you a wider hatred for anything food related.

3) Look for the most expensive gym in your neighborhood and ask for the most all-inclusive, deluxe package you can get. Guilt over the fact that you're not using your gym membership will result in loss of appetite.

4) Throw away your remote control; the resulting back and forth from the couch to the TV should boost your metabolism a good 30 to 35 percent!

5) Five words: William S. Burroughs Heroin Diet.

6) Eat your next meal at a fancy restaurant, like Masa or Per Se; the resulting poverty will keep you from eating for weeks.

7) Start reading about the healthcare industry in America; the resulting pacing around your apartment and angry conversations with conservatives should burn enough calories for at least two workouts. (Warning: this might also result in hair loss.)

8) When you go to the grocery store, bring along a wallet-size picture of Natalie Portman. Every time you approach something delicious look at that picture and remember that you want to have sex again some day.

9) "Reduced fat" is totally meaningless! You might be a schlub, but that doesn't mean you're stupid!

10) Give up. After all, we've all gotta go sooner or later . . .

Chapter Nine*

$

1+1

*Schlub and Taxes

"And so the house came to be haunted by the unspoken phrase: *There must be more money!*"
—D.H. Lawrence, "The Rocking-Horse Winner"

It all started so innocently . . .

I went down to the lobby of my old apartment building and found a letter waiting in the mailbox. I don't remember whether I looked at the return address, but if I did it didn't set off any alarms. There weren't any weird smells emanating from the envelope or dangerous-looking powders sprinkled along the return address. It wasn't especially thick or thin. I just opened it as I headed towards the front door with hardly a thought in my head.

But as I read the letter, I felt the sinking, horrible feeling that you only get when something serious and life changing has just happened, like you found out that you just got some girl "with child." Or that the army finally got around to reinstating the draft, and that you've been chosen as part of the first platoon hitting Baghdad.

"Oh, my God!" I said out loud, even though there was nobody around to hear.

And as my eyes widened and my hands started to shake, I immediately raced back upstairs to my apartment, chanting: "Oh, shit. Oh, shit. Oh, *shit* . . ."

The moment I closed the door I read the letter again. And then I read it a third time.

I called my girlfriend who was not home. Then I called my father who was also not at home.

"Uh, Dad, this is Max," I said, on his machine, my voice cracking. "Please call me back as soon as you get this message."

Then I called my best friend, who was in his final year at Stanford law school.

"Hey. It's me . . ."

"What's wrong?" he said, sensing the distress in my voice.

"I think I'm really fucked . . ."

"Why?" he said. "What?"

I proceeded to read him the letter I had just received. He listened quietly, without comment or interruption. When I finished he pronounced:

"It sounds like you're being audited."

In retrospect, it still seems absurd that an impoverished schlub like me should have wound up in the IRS's crosshairs.

It's a little like sending the U.S. army to take Grenada.

"How did *you* get audited?" my father said when he called me back later that afternoon.

That was pretty much the question everyone else would have when they heard this. (Along with declarations of sympathy along the lines of, "I'd rather be knocked on the head and sold as a galley slave!") Nobody could believe that a man with so little money could have ever attracted government attention.

"I don't know! What am I going to do?"

"Just relax," he said. "You'll call Noah and ask him what to do." Noah was my father's accountant who did my taxes at a cut rate, mostly out of fondness for my father. "This probably happened because you have such an expensive accountant. They must think you're hiding money if you can afford Noah."

My father had been lobbying me to get a cheaper accountant for years.

"Dad!" I cried. "This is not the time!"

"Okay, calm down."

But there was no chance of me being calm. The IRS had said that they wanted an answer within ten days!

They wanted records, and like any self-respecting schlub, I

didn't keep records! (Not good ones, anyway.)

"I'm going to jail," I said, grimly. (Shifting, I might add, from schlubbiness into self-pity.)

"Don't be an idiot. This will be a pain in the ass, but you'll get through it. Stop being a baby."

Noah was also sanguine about the whole thing when I called him a little while later. He assured me that even though I had to contact the case officer within ten days, I would have weeks (months, even) to prepare my audit.

"All right," he said, "drop off the letter they sent you on Monday. You have audit insurance, right?"

Noah offered all of his clients a $50 insurance policy for which he would take care of their audit free of charge if they ever got stuck.

"No."

"Oooh . . ."

He reflected on this for a moment.

"You should have gotten the insurance," he offered.

Yes, I should have.

I had considered it when the offer came up years earlier when I filed my first tax return with Noah. I even brought up the idea to my father. "What are you, crazy?" my father said. "Who's going to audit you?"

The audit is, perhaps, the most punishing thing that can happen to a schlub.

As you know by this point, we are not terribly neat or organized people. I, for one, am a packrat—terrified I might throw out something I would some day need—and thus drowning in completely useless paper.

Every six or seven months, when my apartment becomes so

unbearably cluttered that even I can no longer take it, I make a vow to keep myself better organized and attempt to do something about the heaping stacks of paper that accumulate on (and around) my desk. I'm still a little amazed at the things I've found in those stacks of paper over the years: report cards from grade school; old doggerel I composed in the sixth grade and never threw out. There would be fifteen-year-old birthday cards from my Aunt Rita and even letters from the long gone, like my grandmother, nesting alongside college papers on Descartes and Pascal's wager.

But while these periodic cleanings were certainly useful, they were always temporary solutions. I was never able to remake myself into an organized person. Schlubs just can't. We're not neat in appearance; we're hopeless when it comes to scrubbing down a bathroom or kitchen; and should you ever mention the words, "filing system," we're liable to laugh in your face. (This might explain why my history at *The Forward* was somewhat checkered; as an office manager and personal assistant, my skills were lacking, to put it politely.)

This is the primary reason why the audit is so horrible an ordeal for a schlub. The idea of finding a particular receipt—let alone the hundred or so that this audit called for—seems impossible.

"They want to examine your home office and your 'other expenses,'" Noah said after he reviewed the IRS's letter. "Write up a bio of yourself; say something about the newspapers you've written for, some of the things you write about, that sort of thing. Then collect all the receipts for everything you've deducted for your 'other expenses' . . ."

"Other expenses" included any of the meals I ate for Daniel's magazine. It also meant movies, CDs, and books I might have considered reviewing—as well as anything else I figured was in some way work-related, like newspapers and magazines. My home office was the part of my apartment that was strictly quartered off for work. Noah told me to take photos showing clear demarcations for the home office—and he even suggested I sketch a rough blueprint of the apartment's layout.

"Your office isn't the same as your bedroom, right? You have like a screen up or something separating it, right?"

Pause.

"Right."

"Where do you live again?"

"Bay Ridge."

"And where is the IRS office?"

Downtown Brooklyn.

"Well, if they're close enough, they might stop by for a visit," said Noah. "So make sure that the office is really there."

They might actually visit the apartment? That sounded kind of scary.

"If you don't have receipts, you can't claim the items you deducted. You'll owe them money. But you don't need receipts for under $25. You've been documenting stuff, right? You have a calendar?"

"Uh. Sure . . ."

"Okay," Noah said, "I'll schedule something with this woman from the IRS and you'll come back here the week before and we'll go over everything. You won't have to appear in front of them—I can take care of it myself."

Noah gave me about two months to get everything in order. So I went home and began wading through all that paper.

And aside from the effort of actually finding my receipts (many of which, I was soon to discover, had been expunged during one of my periodic purges), there was the slight humiliation of what I was going to do with the receipts I did have.

Back in my carefree, pre-audit days—when I was less afraid of the IRS than I am now—I was much more footloose and fancy free about what I concluded was work-related. (Almost all writers are. "Work-related" becomes open to interpretation, and most of the writers I know who feel a little freewheeling about some purchase say, "Well, I'll write it off . . .") There were plenty of deductions that seemed perfectly reasonable as I was calculating my return, but felt a trifle embarrassing now that they were being examined in the cold light of day.

For example, there was the tuxedo I had deducted.

A dear friend invited me to her wedding that was "black tie recommended," and so I began asking friends and colleagues where you could rent a tuxedo.

Somebody in my office suggested that I not rent (which would cost a fortune, anyway) but buy one at the Burlington Coat Factory. So one Saturday afternoon, I went down to the new Atlantic Center in Downtown Brooklyn with a pal of mine who was also going to the wedding and found a brand new tuxedo for $178. (And that wasn't even the cheapest one they had!)

As I was looking at different price tags and sizes, it occurred to me that trying to find New York's second cheapest tuxedo was a pretty funny idea for an article. A few months later, a small piece I wrote about the "Best place to get a cheap tux" found a spot in *The New York Press*—and I felt doubly good. Cheap tuxedo; article; and tax deduction—all in one purchase!

But now that I was looking at the receipt (which included another $13 for a tuxedo shirt, and $8 for a bowtie that I had also deducted), I felt a little like a fraud.

Yes—one could argue—I wasn't lying or cheating: this tuxedo

had made a bona fide appearance in an article I wrote, and writing articles was my business. Of course it's a legitimate business expense. But I didn't really need to *buy* the tux to write the story, did I? I felt that in that deduction, I had followed the letter of the law and not the spirit. And I briefly wondered if I hadn't made a horrible mistake in including it. (This might help explain why liberals are such a dying breed; we really do suck at feeling a sense of entitlement.)

And then there were even more embarrassing deductions like "the Benito Mussolini T-shirt"—which was undoubtedly a legitimate expense, but just something shameful to have to explain.

A long time ago, my father had been trolling around Little Italy and found hanging proudly in the window in of one of the crumbling old storefronts on Spring Street a T-shirt which featured Benito Mussolini.

It was not some kind of ironic T-shirt, like the ones that feature Charles Manson, looking extra crazy. (Not that I ever quite understood what was "ironic" about walking around with the picture of a serial killer on your chest.) This was a sincere tribute to Il Duce. Mussolini was portrayed heroically, in an army helmet (which is pretty funny considering what a shitty soldier Mussolini was) and surrounded by red, white, and green bunting. Whoever had designed the shirt was clearly going for a George Washington effect.

My father thought it was hilarious.

So hilarious, in fact, that he bought three—one for himself, one for my mother, and one for me.

I was a freshman at Dartmouth at the time, so when my shirt arrived in the mail, I nearly doubled over with laughter upon opening the package. I told my friends that I now owned an honest-to-goodness piece of fascist propaganda.

And although I'm not one to quibble with the fact that Mussolini was a horrible dictator, a partner of Hitler, and, in general, a menace of a man (who hurt his countrymen and hurt the Allies), there's something about Mussolini that just doesn't inspire the same venom as the other Axis powers do. There was something a little too ridiculous about him to make the shirt offensive. (There was something—dare I say?—*schlubby* in him . . .*)

Lord only knows what happened to that shirt. It somehow disappeared and never turned up. But six or seven years later, when I was invited to contribute to *The New York Press*'s "best of" issue (the same rag I wrote the "best place to find a cheap tuxedo" piece for), I thought the "best T-shirt hanging in a storefront window" had to be—hands down—the Mussolini T-shirt. I went down to Little Italy, found the store that still had it in their window, bought an extra-large, and chatted with the owner about how popular that T-shirt was, exactly.

"Pretty popular," the old Italian shopkeeper admitted. "A lot of people come here specifically for that."

I wrote up the article, and (naturally) deducted the T-shirt on my tax returns.

How was I going to explain that? I could just picture an IRS agent staring at me, blankly, as I tried to explain that, "No, I don't

---

* For the record, Mussolini's time in power was not nearly as innocuous as I suggest. His invasion of Ethiopia was extremely brutal and aggressive (albeit not nearly as disastrous to the Italian army as his invasion of Greece), but there was something so pathetic about the fact that Italian tanks would fall apart when attacked by an unevenly matched Ethiopian resistance. Even an impoverished, third-world nation made Il Duce look like a loser.

approve of Mussolini . . . but it's kind of hilarious that he's turning up on T-shirts, right?" The moment I left her office, I could picture her calling up the FBI and telling them to start a file on the Jewish fascist out in Bay Ridge.

There were plenty of other humiliations, too. I had written about a Mexican restaurant in Park Slope where I had ratcheted up one of the biggest bills of my food reviewing career (the total was well north of $100), and I couldn't find the receipt for it. So, hat in hand, I went to the restaurant to ask if they could give me a copy of my bill. (They said no.) I went to the newsstand where I got my *New York Times* every morning, and tried to explain to the guy behind the counter—the same guy who saw me every morning!—that I needed a note from him saying that this was the place where I got my newspapers. He had no idea what I was talking about.

"You have to speak to the owner," was all he would say.

And then there was the fact that my bank had been sending my bank statements to the wrong address for years—even though I had asked on several occasions for them to correct this. I didn't have a single canceled check.

"What do you mean you don't have any checks?" Noah said when all I could show him was my check register. "Why not?"

"The bank never changed my mailing address," I said. "I've been asking for years."

Noah just stared at me.

"Well, the check register counts for something," he said. "You might get away with it. But I'd go to the bank and try to get your canceled checks back."

My bank—in an act that forever alienated them to me—refused to get me the checks for weeks. Then tried to charge me $600 for the service.

One of the good things about schlubs is that even though we are definitely prone to moments of genuine panic, we quickly drift back into schlubby indifference. Quite honestly, a good movie or a decent meal is enough to turn the tide of our mood and make us think that things aren't as bad as we had thought minutes earlier.

So even though I admit that I started out my audit as a panicky, whiney baby, this did not last long. After a few trips to my favorite Italian restaurant, my fears were somewhat assuaged. And I went about the audit in a state of annoyed indifference rather than complete meltdown. It became more of an ordeal than a matter of my personal freedom being at stake.

The lack of receipts was my biggest problem; so I did my best to estimate dates, times, and places where I had some of the meals I deducted (and said as much in my letter to the IRS). I made Xeroxes and wrote out explanations for every missing receipt. I got so carried away that I wrote out explanations for partial deductions—like entertainment—for which I wasn't being examined. Just in case they asked. ("They *can't* ask!" Noah told me. "They'd have to audit you separately for that. All they can ask about is the home office and the 'other expenses.' ")

When I met with Noah the week before the audit and began going through every sheet of paper, he said, "Max, I gotta tell you: You're as prepared for this as anyone I've ever seen."

I was slightly surprised (as well as mildly touched) by this.

He even gave me one better: "I'll tell you what: I think you can handle this audit without me. If I go down there I'll have to charge you an extra $300—but I think you can explain everything without me. In fact, I think you could probably explain it better than I can. I wouldn't offer to let you go by yourself if I didn't think you could handle it. But I'm happy to go if you want me to. Up to you."

Whoa.

You sometimes wonder about turning points in a life—how you're more competent and well-informed than you yourself suspected you were. I had always assumed that I was a hapless schlub. Was the rest of the world as schlubby as I am?

Given how much I was already spending on the audit (along with whatever correction the IRS asked me to make), I decided to take Noah up on the matter. "Okay," I said. "If you really think I can handle it . . ."

He nodded.

So one winter morning I went down to the IRS's Brooklyn headquarters and sat with a fairly nice, middle aged woman whom I gave my receipts to. And even my auditor told me that I was much more prepared than her typical examination. As I explained to her the sorts of things I wrote about and showed her articles that corresponded to receipts she nodded and looked slightly daunted by the heaps of paper I was presenting.

"Well," she finally said, "we don't have to go over all this together. I can examine it by myself and UPS your receipts back to you."

"Oh. Okay . . ."

"Well, it was nice meeting you," she said.

And that was it. The audit had taken less than an hour.

More strangely, I never got my receipts back—or ever heard from the IRS again. I waited for a few weeks before I called Noah and asked him if I should worry.

"Don't push it," he said. "They'll call you if they need anything."

So I didn't push it.

I called and left a message for the lady who examined me when I filed my income taxes later that spring. "I just wanted to make sure the audit didn't affect my tax return in some way," I said on the machine. Lord only knows if she ever got my message, but I never heard from her.

The hurricane had swept through my life, and I seemed to come out of it without much damage. The schlub can survive these sorts of disasters.

A Schlub and His Money Are Soon Parted:

The Ultimate Schlub's Guide to Avoiding (and Surviving) An Audit

1) Overpay.

Yes, we all fantasize about going into our accountant's office and finding that we will be getting an enormous check back from the government in a few weeks time. I remember the first time it happened to me. It felt pretty goddamned fabulous knowing that in a few short weeks, I would be presented with a check for nearly $2,000. And I even began to think that April would be a fun time of the year—a time when the government gives you money! I couldn't wait for tax season!

But as much fun as it is to get a big check, that feeling wears thin pretty fast—especially in comparison to the uneasy feeling of limbo that you experience with an audit. The audit will be a cloud over your head for months until your IRS officer finally says, "Okay, this looks pretty good." For this reason, I think it's worth not taking a few shaky deductions. Overpay a little bit—that way you'll have wiggle room should the unthinkable happen.

Writers are allowed a lot of deductions; books and CDs and movies are all legit if that's something you're planning on writing about. But don't be a dope. Don't deduct every CD, every book, and every movie you went to see on your return.

2) Get the audit insurance.

Noah was nice to me. He didn't charge an arm and a leg. Most accountants will not be nice to you.

Just do it and don't complain.

3) Keep your receipts.

It sounds like the most obvious thing in the world.

Come to think of it, it is the most obvious thing in the world. You buy something tax-deductible. You save the receipt. You claim it on your return. Makes sense.

However, most schlubs have not yet figured out this extremely simple rule of life.

Before you even finish reading this book, go out to Ikea and buy a file cabinet. Designate one drawer "the receipts drawer." And that's the long and short of it.

And if you can't be bothered to do that, I have an idea for all schlubs out there: Go to the supermarket. Purchase a $2 Tupperware container. Put receipts in it when you get home every night.

Repeat until April 15.

4) Keep your receipts—even after you got your return.

Don't be a schmuck and throw your receipts away after you get your return. Hold on to them for four years.

Duh.

5) Stay away from even numbers.

Call me superstitious, but if you are deducting exactly $4,000 worth of expenses, I believe that there is a machine at IRS headquarters that immediately singles you out for a severe, all-inclusive audit. I believe in staying away from even numbers. Just make it $3,998 and save yourself some possible grief.

6) Don't dress like a schlub when you are hauled before the IRS.

The night before I went to the IRS, I actually wondered which would help my case more: dressing up, or dressing down.

My reasoning went like this: Wouldn't my case officer be more inclined to view me as someone who was really pathetic and hard up if I dressed badly? Maybe that would say to her I didn't even have the money to outfit myself properly and couldn't possibly be hording money. She would therefore go easy on me.

This mode of thinking is incredibly stupid.

You want to appear as un-schlub-like as possible before meeting with your case officer. You want him or her to think that you're treating this audit with the utmost seriousness. That none of your deductions were frivolous. And that you do have the financial resources to fight this should it advance to the next level.

7) The more paper you hand them, the better.

I have no proof to back me up on this rule, but when I showed up with my receipts and more than one hundred sheets of Xeroxes and papers with explanations for every expense that

I had accrued, my case officer looked surprised. And, I think, impressed. (Also a little bit daunted.) Most of the people who had showed up for the meetings at the other desks had no such stacks of paper. (They were also not dressed nearly as well as I was, I should add.)

Writing the explanations, I think, helped immensely. Even if my explanation wasn't good enough to be considered legitimate, I couldn't be accused of bad faith: every expense had an explanation.

8) Do not take an adversarial approach.

Granted, there are people who work in civil service who live to make your life miserable. "I was rude and took pleasure in being so," says the civil servant narrator in Dostoevsky's *Notes from the Underground*.

It's funny because it's true.

But while you can occasionally say, "Fuck you," to the bitchy woman at the DMV or the jerk giving you a hard time at the post office, you'd be wise to be on your best behavior when visiting the IRS. The DMV or the post office can't really harm you. The IRS can. I just smiled, nodded, and was as personable as I knew how to be. (I also benefited immensely from the fact that my case officer was not a spiteful or nasty woman.)

9) Just relax.

If you get the horrible letter from the IRS saying that they want to examine your finances, don't fret too much. As my father used to say to me: "Be a man!" (Or a woman.) It's not the worst thing in the world—it's just a pain in the ass. Unless you're an out and out criminal, you will not go to jail. Worse comes to worst, you pay a fine. Big deal.

10) Do not have breakfast before your audit.
You'll just have to trust me on this one.

*Bugging Out

In what could this flea guilty bee,
Except in that drop it suckt from thee?
—John Donne, "The Flea"

Not too long ago, I met a girl (let's call her Lois) who was bright and beautiful—with chestnut brown hair, and a tiger's glint in her eyes—with whom I quickly fell in love.

One night, when the two of us were alone in her tiny, Cobble Hill studio, I even told her as much.

"Really?" she said.

"You don't have to say it back, if you don't want."

She smiled.

"I can't believe you just said that with the news on," she laughed.

Yes, the TV had been glowing in the background. And I wondered, for a moment, if I had blown it.

But she leaned towards me, put her hand on my cheek and said, "I love you, too."

It was the first time I had ever heard those words before. (Well, that's not entirely true. One girl said it—but it was in the process of breaking up with me, so that doesn't really count.) And that night, as the two of us held each other in our arms, I shed a tear or two of joy.

And while I worried about certain tendencies I have to say or do something stupid in relationships, this one felt different. I wondered if I might be moving out of a schlubby tendency to fuck up an affair, and into a more mature, adult phase of life.

We even began speaking—in a conspiratorial, giddy way—about a future marriage and family. Names of our prospective sons and daughters were discussed with large, uncontrollable smiles. Our grinning and winking wasn't out of any doubts about our life together; it was because the future seemed so alive with promise and happiness. (At least that's how I interpreted it.)

But, alas, Lois and I were not meant to be.

Up until the month that our affair ended (two months past my relationship record) I was publicly stating to friends and colleagues that we would wind up together in the end. Even the week of our breakup, I held out hope. "No," I confessed to my best friend over the phone, "this hasn't been a good week for us. But I still love Lois, and I still think she's the woman I'm going to marry."

Nevertheless, Lois gathered up her nerve and ended things. I was crushed. (And I gained a lot of weight.)

How did this happen? What could have torn a happy, flowering young relationship asunder?

Bedbugs.

Of course, it was a little more complicated than that.

An argument could be made that bedbugs really just brought to the foreground other issues that had been lurking underneath the surface. And I think that there's some truth to this argument.

However, I'm also convinced that our relationship would have gone on a lot longer (and might, indeed, have ended in marriage) if not for bedbugs.

Bedbugs arrived in force in my apartment and when I saw the first one, I didn't think much of it.

For one thing, I didn't know it was a bedbug. It was just a tee-ny, tiny rust-colored disk that was crawling up the bedroom wall, which I quickly killed and washed down the sink.

And even though I always had an aversion to bugs, that first little bedbug seemed harmless. Certainly, it wasn't the kind of thing anyone wanted to see—particularly in the bedroom—but it was small, and easily dispatched, and I had sort of reconciled myself to the fact that my apartment building was a bit crummy, and filled with all sorts of crawly things, anyway.

The previous summer, I had a cockroach infestation that was as disgusting as any kind of horror picture could have made it out to be. Roaches were coming out from behind the baseboards, and from behind the oven; they would turn up in my bathroom and my bedroom at night. I even caught one crawling through my dresser drawers one morning as I looked for a pair of shorts (which completely freaked me out).

One evening when I saw a roach creep out from behind my stove, I immediately grabbed a can of Raid and sprayed him. With a kind of heart-thumping suddenness, six of the roach's brothers came wriggling out from behind the stove all at once. I was so repulsed that after spraying all six of them to death, I fled the scene. I spent the night at an old girlfriend's apartment.

To make a long story short, I hired an exterminator and professional cleaner and got rid of them—giving me the (false) confidence that I could deal with other types of bugs.

Bedbugs, on the other hand, seemed more of a mythical problem than a real one. Bedbugs were something that mothers warned their children about before going to bed: "Don't let the bedbugs bite!" As if there were a tiny army of piranhas under the mattress, waiting to devour.

I was sort of acquainted with the fact that there were real things called bedbugs, but I didn't know anything about them. And I didn't even seem to notice the fact that my legs were covered in bites.

"What are those?" Lois asked one night as I cozied up next to her.

"Uh, I don't know," I said, looking at the little scabs along my leg. "Little scratches, I guess. Maybe from itching? Beats me."

Surprisingly, Lois was satisfied with this response. (At this point, I suppose she figured out that her boyfriend was a bit clue-less and schlubby.) She did not press the matter.

But one night I got into my bed and saw another of those rusty little bugs crawling along my sheets. I killed it and flushed it away. But when I woke up an hour or two later, I saw not one but two of the little suckers in my bed. And for the first time I noticed that my legs weren't scabbed over, but they were leaking little pinpricks of blood.

It seemed strange, to be sure, but schlubs are slow to pick up warning signs. I went back to sleep and when I woke a little while later (I am a bad sleeper), I saw another pair of bugs in the bed.

What the hell was going on?

This was the first time that it even occurred to me that the little insects in my bed might be bedbugs. As I thought about this weird happenstance, I made the unlikely connection between the word "bed" and the word "bug." The next morning, I googled "bedbug" and saw a picture of something strikingly similar to the creatures I had been slaying. Moreover, the symptoms of a bedbug infestation were eerily akin to what I had been experiencing. There would, ex-plained the article I found, be little dots of blood along your sheets. (Yup.) As well as little black dots—which were the bedbug's excre-ment. (Gross! But, yeah, I saw that, too.) And you'd find dozens of little brown spots along the seam of the mattress. I stripped off the sheet to look at the seam, and as I lifted the sheet, yet another bedbug came crawling out into the daylight.

Uh-oh.

"I think I have bedbugs," I said to my mother over the phone.

"Eeew!" she squealed.

My father was even blunter: I was not welcomed in his house as long as there was a possibility of me contaminating it with bedbugs.

"What? Really?"

"Sorry," my father said. "But you're infected, as far as I'm concerned."

And both of them implored me to call my landlord, quickly.

"Okay . . ."

"Do it today, Max," my father said. "Right now."

It was a Sunday morning (Easter Sunday, in fact) and I knew that my landlord would not be in his office to take my call, but I left him a message, anyway. And after I hung up the phone, I turned around and took a look at my bed and tried to imagine the little village of bugs that had been founded in there. With gruesome detail, I pictured all the little bug families that had hitched their wagon to my mattress and built homes for themselves, making large, prosperous bug families.

It was nauseating. I definitely didn't want to sleep on that bed again.

I called Lois.

"Honey, I think I have bedbugs."

She let out a concerned little gasp.

"How did that happen?"

"Beats me. But I was wondering: would it be okay if I stayed with you for a few days while I get this taken care of?"

"Sure."

I hung up and began packing a suitcase.

Lois called me back a few minutes later.

"Are you going to give me bedbugs?" she asked, plainly.

I was taken aback.

"I don't think so . . ."

"Yeah?" she said, "how do you know?"

I didn't know what to say.

"You're not going to put me up?"

There was a long pause.

Lois and I had, indeed, been fighting over non-bedbug related topics in the previous weeks. She was scandalized by a jokey—some might argue sacrilegious—Passover Seder that my parents hosted. (The Seder plate included Paxil, Junior Mints, Metamucil, and two other *Seinfeld*-ian items that I can no longer remember. The Passover prayer was written by my father, and pretty funny as I recall. As Lois and I went home, she said, "Do you guys care that your niece and nephew think that that's really a Passover Seder?") And I admit that a few nights prior to my bedbug discovery, I had a very ugly (and uncharacteristic) display of jealousy that led to a major argument. (For which I apologized profusely.)

"I can't take this," she said. "The audit; the fighting; your job—now bedbugs! Where does it end?"

Oh, yes . . . *The Post* had been dangling a full-time job in front of me for a few months, and it hadn't yet come to fruition. Which, of course, spurned massive bouts of neurotic self-doubt, and lots of whining on my part.

And suddenly—for the first time in our relationship, actually—Lois burst into tears. After she had sniffled for a few seconds she said. "I just can't talk now—I'm going to go." She hung up.

I was stunned. I just sat looking at the phone for a few minutes, wondering if all of those fantasies we had spun together had been phony the whole time. After all, when I thought of marriage vows—for richer or for poorer; for better or worse—I assumed that also included bedbugs.

When I met my parents for lunch that afternoon in Manhattan, my father shook my hand wearing one of those rubber gloves they give out in hospitals.

"Very funny," I said, unamused.

"You don't think that's funny?" he laughed.

"No."

My landlord called me that night and gave me the number for the exterminator. The receptionist at the exterminator's office recognized my voice from the previous summer's cockroaches. "Oooh, Max," she said upon hearing my latest problem, "that's not good. I gotta tell you, if I had to pick between cockroaches and bedbugs, I think I'd go with cockroaches."

"Really?"

"Yeah. Well, we'll send somebody over there sometime this week . . ."

I had to wait three days before the exterminator could visit me. I slept on the couch the whole while (which means I didn't really sleep at all) and when he came he sprinkled white powder (poison) called Tri Die on the floors throughout the apartment. He then went to my mattress, plopped it in the center of the floor, and began spraying it with the smelly, gassy insecticide. As he did this, my little village of bedbugs began pouring out of the mattress. ("Yup," he noted, in case there was any doubt, "you have bedbugs.")

"You should do a few things," the exterminator told me. "First, you should have all your clothing cleaned. Put them in the dryer on high for at least thirty minutes. And check along the seams of any furniture you have."

"They live in clothes, too?"

"Sure."

"What about my books?" I said. "Do they live in books?"

"They can."

I had four bookcases and 1,000 (or more) books in my apartment.

"Go through your books and check for them," he advised.

"Okay . . ."

"Keep the powder on the floor for at least two weeks," the exterminator said.

"Uh, should I be living here? You know, with, like, poison on the floors and everything? Is that healthy?"

He shrugged.

That did not instill me with confidence.

So being that Lois and I were now not speaking, I called my mother and told her that there was poison on my floors and it would have to stay there for two weeks.

"Okay," she said, "you can stay here. But just make sure you wash everything before you come."

I took a bag of laundry to the cleaners, and moved back in with my parents, on their dining room couch.

My parents were not happy to have me back. In fact, as nervous as I was about the bedbugs, my parents were much more terrified.

"You cannot bring them into this house," my mother warned me. "You know your father won't live with them; we'll have to move if we get them, too. And you know that he won't take anything from the apartment with us. It will completely destroy our lives, and we're too old for that to happen to us now."

"I understand."

So I had to accept the fact that as long as I was back with my parents, I would be treated like a leper.

Once I had washed with Prell shampoo (which killed bedbugs according to my father's doctor—lord only knows if that's true), and once I was wearing clothes that had been in and out of the dryer since being in my apartment (sneakers included), only then would I be allowed entry into my parents' house.

This meant stripping down naked in the hallway, putting on a towel, showering, and putting any potentially infected clothes in the wash.

Trunks and suitcases from my old apartment were absolutely forbidden to come with me. Instead I went to Target and came home with a few plastic storage bins, which is where I would put my things once they had been through the washing machine.

The foldout couch I slept on was not particularly comfortable. In fact, it was painfully uncomfortable.

This did not feel like a particularly good moment in this schlub's life . . .

I'm sure that a lot of my readers will be scratching their heads at this point and wondering what, exactly, was the big deal about bedbugs. In fact, I wondered this, too, until I saw how everyone else was reacting and sort of co-opted their hysteria. But, in all fairness to both sides, bedbugs are a major pain in the ass, no matter how sensibly you look at the problem.

It's perfectly true, the damage a bedbug inflicts is relatively minimal. So you get a little bite. So what? The biting isn't any worse than a mosquito. (In fact, it's much better.) People don't react with the same level of hysteria against those pests, do they?

The difference, however, is that bedbugs are notoriously hard to kill. They can shrivel up into white little dots that are barely visible to the naked eye. (The only time they're visible and rust-colored is when they've just sucked your blood!) And they are resilient! They can live for a year without food. (A more pessimistic exterminator I spoke to told me it was two years.) To paraphrase from how Richard Dreyfuss described the shark in *Jaws*: all they do is nest, and drink your blood, and make little bedbugs—and that's it.

And even though I didn't really know enough to be afraid of

bedbugs, nearly everyone else I knew was—not just Lois. Whenever I mentioned this to a friend, they would take a step away from me. (Sometimes jokingly, sometimes not.) Or I would see them looking me over to make sure there was nothing crawling out of my sleeve.

It became as embarrassing to tell people as if I had just been diagnosed with herpes. So I mostly kept it to myself.

And, goodness knows, it promised to be expensive. It was not just the idea of getting all your clothes cleaned—I was paranoid enough to think that every stick of furniture in my apartment was now suspect. Everything that couldn't be cleaned would have to be thrown out. I could only think on the future costs with nervous anxiety.

Plus, in the middle of all of this, there was the fact that Lois and I weren't speaking to each other.

We exchanged a few surly emails before we met up for drinks one night after work.

"Well, all the people I spoke to about this think I'm right," Lois said. "I mean, just because you have this problem why should I inflict it upon myself?"

"Obviously, Lois, I don't want to bring them into your house, too," I said. "And if you said that I had to take precautions to not bring them into your apartment that would be fine. I could understand that. But I was in trouble and I needed a place to go and you said no. That hurts."

(Incidentally, when I asked my friends about this, I got a surprisingly mixed response. Some took my side—some took Lois's. One couple disagreed with each other—in front of me. "I can't believe she turned you away," said the guy. His fiancée looked at him and said, "I wouldn't let you bring those things into *my* house." He looked back at her and declared: "Well, that would be it for us, then, I guess." "You would break up with me over that?" she asked. "Yup.")

Lois clearly felt bad about the situation.

"Well, if you want to stay with me, you can."

Schlubs are rarely proud. I went to my parents house, gathered up my clothes and moved in to Lois' studio, where our relationship lasted for another week.

In all fairness, schlubs are difficult to live with. (See Chapter Three.) The fact that we were living not in a two-bedroom, or even a one-bedroom, but in a studio which measured less than 400 square feet, and only had a bathroom for respite didn't help the matter.

And when you're with a schlub for seven days a week, even women like Lois (who had a clear affinity for schlubs) begin to get annoyed with the small schlubby traits which might have once appeared charming and endearing.

"You should really floss more," she said to me one night as she looked disapprovingly at my mouth. "Your teeth are all yellow. It's disgusting."

I had never heard that criticism from anyone other than a dentist.

We went out to dinner one night, and I mentioned another restaurant that I wanted to visit.

"Is that all you can talk about?" she asked. "Restaurants and food?"

I was hurt. (Especially given my weight worries.) She apologized. But it was clear that she was sick of having me around.

Our living situation came to a head when we went down to Washington one Sunday to participate in a rally to stop the genocide in Darfur. We blew up at each other in the Washington subway, and sat in surly silence along the mall. When we got home that night, she said, "I think you should stay with your parents for a few days."

"Okay . . ."

And when I emailed her the next day to thank her for putting me up and to apologize if I was a burden, she let loose a long email about the pressures I had been inflicting on her. We agreed that it might be wise not to speak for a few days and collect ourselves and our thoughts.

The next week I emailed Lois to tell her I missed her.

"I miss it being fun," she emailed back. "I wish things were different."

Well, that was pretty much the end of that.

There was a perfunctory meeting to officially end the relationship in her apartment. I left her spare set of keys on her kitchen counter and took all the shirts and laundry and books that had accumulated in her apartment and shuffled them into a cab.

"You should call me in a week or so, and we can discuss this further," I said.

She nodded.

I never heard from her again.

But I was as angry as I was saddened by the whole thing. And adding to my anger was the fact that the bedbug situation hadn't really been resolved. The two weeks of leaving the Tri Die on the floors was at an end. I was going to have to get a new bed and clean all the Tri Die up—which I didn't relish doing. I called a professional cleaning company who said that they would do a thorough job—and had special equipment to take care of problems like bedbugs—but it would cost $600.

I said okay.

As the day of the cleaning approached, I wondered if I had made a big mistake. Maybe it was foolish to ever go back to the apartment. The exterminator had told me that he had been in the building a month earlier to treat another of the apartments that had been infested with bedbugs (which was no doubt how I got them). What was the point of doing a thorough cleaning if I was going to leave in a few weeks anyway?

When the cleaner showed up with just a vacuum cleaner (and was surprised—and even nervous—to learn that the apartment had been infested with bedbugs) I sent her away and decided that I would never spend another night in that apartment again.

Moreover, I had in the weeks of this crisis, become something of an expert on bedbugs.

I had read almost every article that I could find about the epidemic (it had a resurgence in recent years). And I began calling up exterminators and even professors of entomology to ask them their advice.

"Your exterminator put Tri Die down?" said one exterminator. "That's dangerous stuff."

I called 311, which said that they would send a city official out to investigate.

Another exterminator told me that putting down poison doesn't do anything unless you're living in the apartment; bedbugs don't come out at night if they can't sense a warm body. I had done nothing to improve my apartment, he said.

"I can come out there and treat the place, but it's only on the condition that you stay there for two weeks. Otherwise, it won't work," he said. "It'll cost about $800—depending on the size of your apartment."

But I was no longer interested in going back to my apartment, just saving as much of my stuff as possible.

I read that bedbugs couldn't stand extreme temperatures, so I began freezing all my books for twenty-four hours. (I began an email correspondence with an extremely kind professor of entomology at Cornell named Dr. Jody Gangloff-Kauffman, who had written one of the foremost articles on bedbugs; Dr. Gangloff-Kauffman told me that she thought freezing was a good idea.) I would come into the apartment, empty the books out of the freezer, put another batch in the freezer, and leave. I spent hundreds of dollars getting every stitch of clothing I ever owned cleaned. Stacks of plastic containers began building up in my parents' foyer.

"This was like a biblical plague," my mother said, "against sloth."

"No!" I shouted. "Sloth and messiness and cleanliness have nothing to do with it. The bedbugs don't come from dirt! Haven't you been reading this stuff?"

Apparently, they hadn't been reading it as rigorously as I had. Until the end of my bedbug crisis, my parents remained convinced it was my comeuppance for a schlubby lifetime spent ignoring things like cleanliness.

I began dreaming about bedbugs at night; horrible dreams in which I would find them in my clothes and my hair and bed. I refused to sit down on the subway because of the prospect of one microscopic bedbug getting into my clothes. I refused to sit down in anybody's house if they had what looked like used furniture. I refused to go into any restaurant that looked as if it might be anything short of immaculate in terms of pests. I vowed that I would never buy another used book—or used anything, for that matter. (Not that anyone had a realistic chance of "catching bedbugs" from any of these things. A hotel bed is much more dangerous.)

When I thought I saw a bug bite one morning, I nearly burst into tears. The problem would never go away. Never. Never. Never . . .

"I would take a million tax audits over this," I stated.

"Yes, this is like being stricken with cancer," my mother agreed.

"Well, maybe not cancer, but something really, really bad."

True, cancer was worse. So was AIDS. And Ebola. But I began going through in my mind all the diseases I would rather have than bedbugs—and the list was pretty long.

You could say I had gone slightly crazy.

In retrospect, I'm somewhat surprised at how long it took me to realize I had gone insane.

Granted, there are degrees of insanity. I certainly wasn't in the talking-to-the-wall variety. I hadn't even reached the 9/11-was-a-government-plot level of paranoia. I was just a normal there-are-bugs-everywhere-that-are-trying-to-get-me sort of nut. But I wasn't *completely* around the bend; I never lost sight of the fact that, no, the bugs weren't after *me*, specifically. I just believed that they could be hiding anywhere, and that I needed to be constantly vigilant.

But my craziness did, eventually, ease up.

One afternoon, my editor asked me if I wanted to go down to Starbucks, and as we sat down with our coffees, he offered me a full-time job. (I took it.)

And I began looking for an apartment.

One Saturday, I answered an ad for an apartment out in Jackson Heights that was a spectacular 800-square-foot one-bedroom, only forty minutes or so from work. (At least twenty minutes faster than Bay Ridge.) The building had a courtyard and the apartment was freshly painted and roomy.

"I'll take it," I said to the husband-and-wife landlords, Eleanor and Larry. (Who were also the next-door neighbors.)

"Think about it overnight," said Larry.

"Okay."

I got my mother to come out and take a look at the place and we both agreed; it was perfect. I moved in the next weekend. (And haven't been back to Bay Ridge since.)

The apartment was almost too big. I had left all my furniture behind, save for a couple of chairs. Even after swabbing my dining room table with a special pesticide that Dr. Gangloff-Kauffman recommended, I decided against taking it with me at the last minute. (Was it worth a second infestation? Or even worrying about a second infestation? Not really, no.)

But I had an apartment all to myself, and that was nice.

And eventually, my bad dreams about bedbugs started to die down. It's true, though that I categorically refused to unpack things unless they had spent at least twenty-four hours in the freezer. (Even six months later, I brought a girl over—who knew my bedbug agony—and when she looked in the freezer she saw it was filled with books. Which she said was one of the weirdest things she had ever encountered in a Maytag.) And it's also true, I could no longer sit in ratty movie theaters or restaurants any more without some nervousness. But I had more or less returned to normalcy.

About three months into my new life in Jackson Heights, I got a call from a friend who said that he had the perfect girl for me to meet.

"This is a great match," my friend said.

"Oh, yeah?"

"Yeah! She had bedbugs, too!"

I considered this for a moment.

"What are you, crazy?" I said. "There's no way anybody with bedbugs is ever coming in my house! Ever!"

Epilogue

One Saturday morning, about a year ago, my father called me up and asked me which movie he and my mother should see that afternoon.

"I don't know," I said. "This movie, *Knocked Up*, has been getting good reviews."

I had been a little wary about recommending *Knocked Up* to him. He hadn't liked *The 40-Year-Old Virgin* (which I had been unexpectedly taken with). Both he and my mother had thought it was too raunchy for them, and the moment I said the words "Knocked" and "Up", I thought this one promised to be equally vulgar. (With a title like that, how could it be otherwise?)

"Who's in it?" he asked.

"Seth Rogen."

"Who's that?"

"He's a young guy. Hasn't been in much. He looks a lot like me."

"Really?"

"Yeah," I said. "It's kind of scary, actually. Anyway, I haven't seen it yet, but it's on my list."

When he and my mother called me later that afternoon, they could barely contain their excitement.

"This guy isn't *like* you," my father exclaimed. "This guy *is* you! And his whole crew is exactly like yours. This is what you guys must have been like when you were in college."

Even though I liked Rogen in the few things I had seen him in, I wasn't exactly flattered to be grouped together with such a schlub. "We're not exactly alike," I said.

"No," my father insisted. "You guys are *exactly* alike."

I have to admit, this did not make me feel very good at the time.

But then I saw the movie—perhaps the greatest love letter to schlubbiness since *Oblomov*. I was equally enchanted.

I saw Rogen's trajectory as similar to mine; while he remained schlubby to the end, he had also cleaned up his life. He had found a job; he had gotten an apartment; he had become responsible. And I had more or less done the same thing; my apartment was now bedbug-free. I had a steady job. I was treating life with some measure of seriousness.

And the similarities between Rogen and myself (not just looks-wise) were so pronounced, that I thought all those dew-eyed girls in the theater who saw in him a loveable schlub, would look at me in the same longing way. This was the impetus behind me remarking in an offhand sort of way to my friend at *The Post*, "There's no question that Seth Rogen is going to improve Max Gross's sex life . . ."

The subsequent article I wrote proved to be the most popular thing I had ever written.

Granted, the stories I wrote for *The Post* were largely real estate articles, and most people can't work up the same enthusiasm for real estate that they can for personal stories. But old friends and acquaintances were stunned to see their schlubby comrade given such grand treatment. A picture of me appeared on the cover of *The Post*'s "Pulse" section, with a beautiful blonde (the writer Mandy Stadtmiller) on my arm.

My in-box was crammed that morning with emails from people I hadn't heard from in years; from real estate publicists who had no idea that I was also funny; from classmates now living in other cities; even from ex-girlfriends who wanted to tell me how hard they laughed. (There was no message from Lois, but I wasn't really expecting anything.) When I went to *The Forward* offices later that day (I had been invited to a going-away party for a friend of mine), I was cheered. I had won one for the schlubs.

My friend Julian Voloj gave the article to a friend of his at work. She left the article on his desk with a post-it note that read, "I [heart] him."

"Maybe you guys should get together," Julian said to the girl. "I mean, you're funny and he's funny. You're a writer, he's a writer . . ."

Email addresses were exchanged. A date was made.

Mary (the girl) and I met up in the East Village for coffee and dessert one afternoon. And coffee went so well that we walked uptown until it was dinnertime. We ate and kept walking until we hit Central Park.

Our lips were locked by the end of the night. (They've pretty much been locked ever since.)

And Mary—who is extremely beautiful and wickedly intelligent—is also a little disorganized and schlubby about her life.

"We're a schlubby couple," Mary stated after we decided that we had reached the point where we should call ourselves boyfriend and girlfriend. "We're a schluple."

"Agreed."

We've been an extremely happy schluple. After three months,

we each admitted that we were in love, and since then not a day has passed when we didn't say in a frantic, breathless voice, "Oh, honey! I love you!" *

And if there is any great lesson that can be gleaned from the life of a schlub, it is that one shouldn't run away from one's schlubbiness. One should embrace it. Inside every schlub, there's a shtud.

Er, stud.

---

* Naturally enough, between the editing and printing phase of this book, my girlfriend managed to break up with me. (Of course, if you're a savvy reader, you knew that was coming.) But clocking in at more than eleven months, it was one of my longer, more mature relationships. I have plenty of faith that the schlub and stud side of me will some day lure another hottie into caring about me.

Acknowledgments

.

I always thought that Acknowledgments were the way that authors got their chance to give an extended Academy Awards speech. A lot of preening and politicking. Who needs it...?

It turns out that's only half true.

Yes, I'd like to thank all the schlubs out there who stepped in that puddle before I did. This book is their book as much as anybody's. But while writing this book, I started realizing just how many people were helping me along the way. A lot of non-schlubs are to blame for the finished product and they should be acknowledged here.

The germ for this book began when I jokingly remarked to my colleagues at *The Post*, Mandy Stadtmiller, Reed Tucker and Mackenzie Dawson, "There's no question that Seth Rogen is going to improve Max Gross's sex life..."

"Oh, you should totally write that up!" Mandy exclaimed. The other two nodded in agreement. My thanks to all three of them. Stephen Lynch thought enough of the idea to make it the lead story in *Pulse* two days later. (Mandy also wrote a counterpoint to my article that, I concede, was pretty hilarious.)

There are plenty of other people at *The Post* to whom I owe my station and should likewise be thanked. My career there began when my friend Lisa Keys told me about an opening at the paper, and Alison Rogers and Andy Wang were good enough to give me a chance. All three were great friends as well as great colleagues—and I'd be remiss if I didn't also thank my colleague and friend, Jennifer Ceaser, who is also one of the sharpest editors I know.

And, as long as we're veering into Academy Awards territory, there are plenty of people at *The Forward* who gave me my start and showed me how to be a journalist—particularly Andrew Silow-Carroll, Ami Eden, Alana Newhouse, and Daniel Treiman. Aliza Phillips not only first took me on as an intern, but gave me The Hapless Jewish Writer column, and both Gabriel Sanders and Sarah Kricheff have kept me writing for *The Forward*. It was J. J. Goldberg who hired me full-time as a reporter/assistant, and when I was having trouble with the opening of a story, he imparted to me the one lesson every journalist should learn: "Just say what you mean." It's the best advice any writer could ever get. Wayne Hoffman not just turned me into a better writer, but he also consistently pushed me to become more ambitious—and gave me the much needed kick in the tush described in these pages. Thank you, Wayne.

When "Schlub you the Right Way" appeared, Charlie Lyons called me and told me that I might have a book in that article. His brother, Tony Lyons, gave the book the go-ahead and teamed me up with Ann Triestman, who has been as gentle and as encouraging an editor as any writer could ever want. Her assistant Kathleen Go, and Skyhorse's publicist Jennifer Hobbs have proved a true delight to work with.

My thanks to Christian Johnston, who took the photos for this book (and who also provided me with the "Max, you're in hell," diagnosis) and Mia Johansson who posed with me when we needed a "hot blonde" for the cover art. Thank you, Mia! And Carissa Alden deserves my thanks for putting me in touch with Avery Cardoza. My thanks to Matthue Roth for helping me set up this web site: www.fromschlubtostud.com.

My Godfather, Arthur Schwartz and his partner Bob Harned, were good enough to feed me and listen to my ranting on the phone during the writing of this—they were also good enough to let me cancel a vacation to Italy with them so I could finish the book. Thanks guys!

And even though she has a prominent place in the book, I don't think I will ever be able to express my gratitude to Dr. Jody Gangloff-Kaufmann. Dr. Gangloff-Kaufmann: You have no idea how much you helped me overcome my bedbug crisis. My sincerest thanks. Likewise, Noah Kimerling guided me through my audit in one piece—thanks pal. As for Dr. Darryl Isaacs: Thank you for scaring the shit out of me about my health... it was the right thing to do.

Noah Phillips read the manuscript and gave me great notes and encouragement. ("You're insane if you don't talk about your relationship with tuna," was Noah's quote, more or less.) And he has been perhaps the best non-professional psychoanalyst a friend could have. He endured many, many late night calls from a fretful schlub and he braved them all with grace and wisdom.

My friends Lisa Keys and Julian Voloj also read the unfinished book and gave me excellent advice... they also fixed me up with my girlfriend, Mary, so it goes without saying: You two are tops.

Of course, Mary Ought Six was the most loving girlfriend any guy could ask for during the writing and editing of this book. Not only was she (rightly) insistent that I have a social life outside of writing, but she also went through the manuscript with a red pen, found mistakes, made changes, and overall made the book far better. She is a wonderful woman whom I love very deeply, and I am very grateful to her.

Two slightly more ruthless editors, however, were my mother and father. They got the first look at everything and they were never afraid to tell me where and when I had gotten off track. ("It's shit," is their most memorable—and most frequent—criticism of any of my writing.) But if nobody was harder on me, nobody was a greater fan and champion. It is to them that this book is dedicated.